99

Before®... Marketing

on the Internet

Your Guide to Setting Yourself Up to
Succeed Online

Peggy McColl

www.99-series.com

The 99 Series
600 Brunet
Montreal, QC H4M1X8
Canada
323-203-0548

The author has done his/her best to present accurate and up-to-
date information in this book, but he/she cannot guarantee that the
information is correct or will suit your particular situation.

This book is sold with the understanding that the publisher and the
author are not engaged in rendering any legal, accounting or any
other professional services. If expert assistance is required, the
services of a competent professional should be sought.

First published by The 99 Series 2010

Ginger Marks Cover designed and Layout by
DocUmeantDesigns *www.DocUmeantDesigns.com*

Copy Edits by **Nancy Peske**
http://NancyPeske.com

Distributed by DocUmeant Publishing
For inquiries about volume orders, please contact:

Helen Georgaklis
99 Book Series, Inc.
600 Brunet Avenue
Montreal, Quebec
Canada
H4M 1X8

Helen@99-series.com

Printed in the United States Of America
ISBN-13: 978-0-9866923-9-0 (paperback)
ISBN-10: 0986692395

WORDS OF PRAISE
FOR...

---

99 Things You Wish You Knew Before®... Marketing on the Internet

"WOW! This is the most complete, no-nonsense and true-to-life guide to Internet marketing I have seen. There's no hype here, just the critical truths that every marketer must know. This is it; this is the ultimate Internet marketing book!"
—**Steve Lowell,** *founder and President of Your Stage Training and Education Inc. and Lowell Workshops*

"Look no further! Peggy's 99 Things book is the complete guide to help build your solid foundation for online success! If you incorporate only a

fraction of these strategies, you will be amazed at the results."—**David Riklan,** *Founder & President of SelfGrowth.com*

"I've known Peggy for a few decades and I've watched her career and business flourish and she makes things happen. Coming from total integrity, she has this gift for distilling complicated things down to the simplest wisdom. If you follow her guidance you can only win at this game of making money online."—**Brian Proctor,** *President of InsightofTheDay.com*

"At last a high quality reference book for all Internet marketers, regardless of what stage they are at. I just wish this had been available when I got started on line. This is one of those rare books that you will dip into time and time again for help and advice."—**Garry Booton,** *Creator of http://homeeasyearn.com*

"If I had only known five of the 99 Things that Internet book marketing mastermind Peggy

McColl reveals in this book, it would have saved me, and the authors I work with, hundreds of hours and hiccups. If you don't get the power of the Internet, Social Media and the direct connection to book marketing success, you are in trouble. Peggy is here to bail you out. I will be recommending this book to all our members and clients."—**Judith Briles, *Founder of Author U(niversity) and TheBookShepherd.com***

"One of the best things you can do for yourself and for your business, if you want to succeed, is to study this book! Within these pages is the most complete source for Internet marketing secrets covering all of the essential elements to help you succeed in a big way."—**John Assaraf, *New York Times Best-selling author, <u>The Answer and Having It All</u>***

"Often times your questions keep you in a marketing paralysis as you spend all your time trying to find the answers. Wouldn't it be nice to have a resource guide that contained the solutions and answers before you even entered into the on-line marketing craze? Well here it is! Every essential

piece of information needed for a successful on-line marketing experience is contained within the pages of this valuable book that Peggy McColl has put together from years of coaching some of today's most successful, effective on-line marketers of our time. This will be the first book I recommend to any human being who is interested in gaining PhD knowledge in online marketing delivered in an easy to follow and apply format."—
Lauren E Miller, *Stress Relief Expert/Best Selling Author /International Speaker* *www.laurenemiller.com*

DEDICATION

This book is dedicated to those people who are pursuing their dream—and making a positive contribution to the lives of others.

CONTENTS

CHAPTER 5

CHAPTER 6

ABOUT THE 99 SERIES

The 99 Series is a collection of quick, easy-to-understand guides that spell it all out for you in the simplest format; 99 points, one lesson per page. The book series is the one-stop shop for all readers tired of looking all over for self-help books. The 99 Series brings it all to you under one umbrella! The bullet point format that is the basis for all the 99 Series books was created purposely for today's fast-paced society. Not only does information have to be at our finger tips... we need it quickly and accurately without having to do much research to find it. But don't be fooled by the easy-to-read format. Each of the books in the series contains very thorough discussions from our roster of professional authors so that all the information you need to know is compiled into one book!

We hope that you will enjoy this book as well as the rest of the series. If you've enjoyed our books, tell your friends. And if you feel we need to improve something, please feel free to give us your feedback at www.99-series.com.

Helen Georgaklis
Founder & CEO, 99 Series

PREFACE

I will flat out admit that I do not know every-thing about marketing on the Internet. That may seem like an odd statement to read so early in a book... especially a book about 99 Things You Wish You Knew Before Marketing on the Inter-net, but I'm here to tell you my friend, that is actually good news.

You, too, don't have to know everything about marketing online. One of the reasons why people are paralyzed and don't take action is simply because they don't know what to do. Or, they become familiar with many strategies but really don't know where to begin. What I can offer you is what I've learned about Internet marketing that has worked not only for me but also for my many very satisfied clients.

I started marketing on the Internet, and I mean really marketing on the Internet, in the early

2000s. I had set up my Web site in 1996, but that original site was more like a brochure than anything else, and I didn't do any business through it. Up until the year 2002, people couldn't buy anything from my Web site. Did that mean that my Web site wasn't serving a purpose? No, because it functioned well as a static advertising piece. It wasn't until I discovered that we can reach people anywhere in the world with our expertise by way of products and/or services that I changed my business model and saw my revenue shift in a significant upward motion.

In the process of learning all that I know about Internet marketing, I made some mistakes. I took some risks that didn't pan out, and others that did—some far beyond my expectations. Now I can look back and share with you strategies that have proven to be successful, and warn you about the challenges that you'll face (and how to avoid the costly ones) as you begin to invest time and money in doing Internet marketing. I hope my lessons, hard-earned, are of the greatest possible value to you!

ACKNOWLEDGMENTS

First and foremost, the person who needs to be acknowledged the most in this book is my sister Judy O'Beirn. She should probably have her name on this book, as a co-author because she was instrumental in helping me organize the structure and pull together the content, and she meticulously reviewed the chapters to ensure the reader would receive great value. With a tight deadline to complete the manuscript on time, Judy dropped everything, drove to my home (a five-hour drive) and stayed up with me almost around the clock while we completed the work that needed to be done to have a manuscript ready for editing. Judy, I'm grateful for your support and wisdom. To Judy's husband Gerry O'Beirn, I'm grateful for your being so willing to jump in to support the book as well, do the drive back and forth, and for being so kind and generous to make sure anything we needed was available for us (water, coffee, more coffee, food and more coffee).

To my husband, Denis, who is always flexible, loving, and supportive, I'm grateful. Denis is the rock in my life. He inspires me with his easy-going, kind nature. I'm grateful for Denis' love, unwavering support in my career as an author, and for his support for my businesses.

My son, Michel, is my biggest inspiration and everything I do is with Michel in mind. Grateful doesn't even begin to describe the positive emotions I feel for my son whom I love unconditionally.

Nancy Peske, who has ghostwritten many of my other books, jumped in, dropped everything, and with her total grace, talent, and warmth, edited the entire manuscript in record time. I'm completely impressed with Nancy's tremendous talent. I truly believe she is one in a million. I'm grateful to have her in my life and grateful to have her magic touch on this book.

Gay Hendricks, my friend, my mentor and a business partner with me on The Center for Viral Marketing, inspires me by his presence. If you looked up these three words in the dictionary you would find Gay's photo: "giving," "wise," and "integrity." Gay, thank you for your constant and never-ending support, guidance, and friendship.

I also feel so much gratitude for my mastermind buddy and best friend Arielle Ford. Arielle is adored, appreciated, and loved. Arielle and I have a special girlfriend bond unlike other friendship-bonds. I'm so grateful for Arielle as she keeps me accountable every day as we both stay true to our priorities and our "accomplishment" lists.

To my friends who are always supportive in all that I do: David Riklan, Brian Proctor, John Assaraf, Tara Taylor, Linda Crombie, Jennifer Gibson, Lisa Larter, Heather Pardon and Yvonne Higham

To all my clients from around the world whom I am blessed to serve!

And, to my loving and devoted agent, Cathy Hemming. Thank you for being nothing short of outstanding!

Thank you to Michael Wells and Helen Georgaklis for putting together The 99 Series. If it wasn't for you, this book and the many others in the series wouldn't be possible.

With warmth, love and appreciation,

Peggy

INTRODUCTION

I was wounded by the dot bomb era. Prior to working full time in my own business I was a Vice President of Corporate Development, working in the Office of the President for a dot.com international company, and then one day "poof"... unemployed, no regular paycheck coming in, and no severance package. It was a rough awakening.

When I dusted myself off, I decided my next move was to pursue my passion. In my spare time, I had been studying self-help. I seemed to have an unquenchable thirst for information on personal growth. For almost two decades, I had dreamed of working in the self-help field although I wasn't sure what exactly I might do to make money. Six years before finding myself unemployed, I dipped my toe in the water of personal growth and development: I incorporated my business Dynamic Destinies, Inc. The purpose of the business was to offer personal and professional development seminars to both the public and the private sector. I was working in my business part-time on and off for six years. Unemployment gave me the opportunity to devote one hundred percent of my undivided attention to my passion.

As good as my intentions were I did not have a clear plan. I did not know how I was going to produce revenue. I relied heavily on instinct to guide me. I felt very strongly that the perfect revenue-producing opportunities would come my way and my business would be generating income and even profits in record time—but that was not my experience.

At the time, I was a single mother and the sole provider for my household. My son was in private school and I did not adjust my lifestyle to carefully manage the money that I did have before more money came in. I knew I needed to work harder and smarter to create success.

Soon, I decided I would write a book called <u>On Being...The Creator of Your Destiny</u>. I felt the world needed a book that would help people recognize their creative potential and that would deliver important principles about creativity in a simple-to-understand, easy–to-follow text.

I didn't know anything about the book industry. In fact, I didn't know anything about writing a book. And I certainly didn't know how to effectively market on the Internet.

I realized very quickly that there are other people who have created great success and, following the advice of many of my teachers, I decided to "model" success. I found others who were achieving the results that I wanted, paid attention to what they were doing, took action, and followed through. By the time I started generating new revenue in my business, a year-and-a-half had passed. I was a quarter of a million dollars in debt. Needless to say, I was very scared! I knew I had to turn things around and get into the black. I was keeping up with all of my financial obligations but I was dangerously close to being totally tapped out of money and credit. Fortunately, things did turn around fairly quickly once I began to learn how to effectively use the tool of the Internet to market my services and products including my book.

Two weeks after I launched <u>Your Destiny Switch</u>, the book made it onto the New York

Times best-seller list. My publisher told me that Your Destiny Switch was one of the top 10 selling books for them for the year. I then asked the foreign rights director, *"Has anyone inquired about buying foreign rights for my book?"* and she said, *"We've already sold the rights to 8 countries and I've had 3 more inquiries."* I was stunned to hear that there had been so many sales in a matter of weeks and asked her how that happened so quickly. She told me it was as a result of my Internet marketing and promotion.

I am no genius, but I have always worked hard and thought through what my plan is. I work with integrity and self-honesty, and don't allow myself to pretend that something's working when it isn't. I believe that successful people do the things that unsuccessful people aren't willing to do. They persevere when times are tough, ask hard questions of themselves, are honest about their weaknesses, and build upon their strengths. I also believe wholeheartedly that I was not put on this earth to make as much money as possible at any cost. From what I have seen, the people who are the most successful and who enjoy the most abundance are the ones who have their priorities straight and who operate from a sense of purpose and with integrity. I am not out to "get" all that I can from my customers but to make a positive contribution to the lives of millions of others. Knowing that this is my foundation for my business, I am able to follow my passion without compromising my integrity or values. The money I make allows me to provide even more value to my customers, and I truly enjoy what I do every day.

Because I am in business to serve others, I find myself blending the personal with the professional. My reputation as the face behind Dynamic Destinies, Inc. matters to me. I have shared with my clients my son's graduation from high school, the news of my marriage, and the story of losing my mother to cancer after caretaking for her for many months. People shared my joys and sorrows and told me, *"You are so real!"* I believe the personal connection to your customers is more important than ever and, as you learn in the book, you can use modern technology in many ways to make that connection.

CHAPTER 1

THE MOST IMPORTANT DRIVING FACTORS IN SUCCESSFUL INTERNET MARKETING

There are certain "driving factors" that will contribute to and accelerate your online marketing success—and your life for that matter. After all, your business is an extension of you. If it is built on the same solid foundation and values that underlie the way you operate in the world, you will never feel a conflict between who you are as a person and who you are as a professional running a business. Your driving factors are the values that inspire you and keep you going no matter what the challenge. It would be important to know what those driving factors are early in the game, as your entire experience will be so much more enjoyable (and, likely, more *profitable*) if you do.

#1: You Have to Love What You Do

I'm extremely grateful that I happen to love what I do because I know if I didn't I would have given up a long, long, long time ago. When I incorporated my business Dynamic Destinies, Inc., I was driven by passion. It was my desire to make a positive contribution in the lives of millions of others. Even though that may have seemed like a bold statement, and I had no idea how I would achieve this lofty goal, I set the intention anyway.

My own journey of self–discovery took me from a very insecure, frightened young woman to a confident and successful businesswoman, and it was fueled by a passionate study of personal development. I was 19 years old when I was introduced to the world of self-help by a wonderful speaker by the name of Bob Proctor. Bob Proctor opened my eyes to what was possible and at a young age I began to study personal development with as much intensity and devotion it was as if I were going for an honors level degree in the most difficult university program. I began to experience positive change in my life, and before too long, I firmly declared "one day I will work in the field of personal development!" I loved how the books, speakers, workshops, and audiotapes had changed my life and I wanted to help other people experience a positive change in their lives, too.

Your passion might be something entirely different. It might even be a passion for making money, but in the end, you know that money is only a tool for achieving what else you desire. What good would it do to generate enough wealth to buy the boat of your dreams only to be working so many hours that you never had a chance to enjoy it?

If you have heard there's plenty of money to be made marketing on the Internet, know that it's true, but don't feel you must sell the "hottest" type of product or service that's out there regardless of whether it ignites your own passion. Trust that you can make money marketing something that truly ignites your passion. It is much easier to sell what you think is of great value than to sell what someone else thinks is of great value but which leaves you feeling lukewarm or empty. The one time in my life I was let go from a job, I had been trying to sell a product that was pretty good but not great, and I just hadn't been able to muster the kind of infectious enthusiasm needed to make others sit up and take notice of the product. You can sell just about anything on the Internet. Don't settle for something that you're not excited about.

#2: Having a Genuine *Passion* for Your Idea/Business Will Keep You Going in Challenging Times

At this point in my life I have invested three decades studying personal growth. I've invested tens of thousands of dollars going to events and seminars, purchased thousands of books and audio programs, and spent money I didn't have on self-improvement products because I knew they would help me turn my life around. Even though I now have several books and multiple products, and I do speaking engagements all over the world, I still continue to study. I do this not because I'm insecure about what I know but because I can't get enough of the subject I am passionate about. I want to offer my customers even greater value year after year and I know that by continuing to educate myself, I am constantly increasing my expertise.

You will know if you love something by the way you feel about it. You will know you are passionate when you know you *love* it! Do you study a particular field far more than the average person might? Do you make every effort to attend the events in your industry, even though you may not be in the best financial position to get there? Do you talk about your subject area at every occasion? When you find someone else who loves the same genre/industry/field that you do, do you feel a surge of energy inside you? It's easy to determine whether you really love something or not—just connect to how you feel inside.

When the top bloggers began writing their blogs, very often they had no specific intention of eventually netting a book contract or making money-selling products. They simply had to express their thoughts and feelings about a subject dear to their hearts. That passion can keep anyone talking about and learning about her field, sometimes late into the night, regardless of whether her passion is generating any revenue for her yet. There are no reliable ways to make a "quick buck" on the Internet. Passion is what will keep you going when the work is hard and even te-dious. Know how strong your interest is and you won't peter out when the going gets tough.

#3: It's Okay to Decide This Isn't What You Want to Do

When I first incorporated my business, Dynamic Destinies, Inc., I started putting together corporate seminars. I developed and delivered my own programs on subjects such as Customer Service, Team Building, Effective Presentation Skills, and other such "soft" skills. The reason I offered these types of programs is because I felt there was a need for them in the marketplace. Was there a need? Yes, but I quickly discovered that delivering them bored me.

Because I was bored, I became distracted. I really only wanted to invest my time in the personal development industry. If only I could make money selling programs on subjects that truly excited me! As it turns out, I could. However, I had to let go of the idea that I had to sell products I saw a clear need for and instead trust that, with research, I'd find the market for products I was passionate about creating and selling. I had to value my passion and have a little faith that others would share my interest. I could see from the success of other personal development products and services that there was a market for what I wanted to sell, but I also knew that I would have to come up with my own brand, work hard, and be willing to start at the beginning of a learning curve. As much as I could deliver a Team Building seminar in my sleep, I found it difficult to discipline myself to put a great deal of energy into a business based on corporate seminars. The business I'd created wasn't sustainable given my lack of enthusiasm. I had to put the effort into creating, marketing, selling and delivering something I loved.

#4: You Must Keep Your Head about You When Your Emotions Are Taking Over

It is very easy to lose sight of the important aspects of creating a successful business, especially the need to generate revenue when you are pursuing your passion. There are times when I am delivering a keynote speech and I'll announce to the audience that I'm an addict. I'll hear "oooh's" and "ah's" and a rush of silence will come over some of the audience members who are shocked by my frank revelation. But, then I'll continue and explain that I'm an addict for the things I love. While I work in a field I'm passionate about, I have also learned that I need to keep my eye on the revenues and profits of my business.

I like to say, "If you are in business, and you are not doing business (in other words, *making money*), you will quickly be out of business."

You might absolutely love your topic but the number of people willing to spend money pursuing that passion might be too small for you to be able to sell your products or services. Sometimes, by casting a wider net, such as looking to international customers or to customers who are of a different demographic than your own, you might find that there are potential buyers after all. Or, you need to learn how to do better marketing. However, you should always be aware of the difference between a hobby and a business. A hobby is mostly about having fun and enjoying yourself (and sometimes about making money). If you can have fun and turn a profit by creating a business, marketing something related to your hobby, great. But if after doing your research, you see there isn't much money to be made selling products or services to the small number of people who have interest in you and your products, listen to your head and keep your hobby a hobby.

#5: Your Passion Can Change

I will say however, that almost a decade after I started Dynamic Destinies, Inc., with the clear intention to offer personal and professional development programs, I discovered a second passion: Internet marketing. Your initial passion may change or expand, too, as it did for me. Never feel stuck selling what you have always sold.

You may not be certain there's a need for the products/services you'd most like to create and sell. Stick with it, be persistent and you may even need to take a risk. Be willing to research the market and learn who might be your ideal customer. You might be surprised at how big your "niche" is once you start looking closely at the marketplace and its needs.

When I first started marketing on the Internet, my results were positive. I began by marketing my first book using effective Internet marketing strategies. Within a short period of time, my books were being sold into many countries all over the world. Requests for media interviews started to come in, foreign rights publishers started to call me, and my bottom line improved significantly. I was finally making money! One book lead to a self-published second book, and then a third book, and before long, I was also selling and delivering online e-courses (an e-course, or electronic course, is delivered solely over the Internet). Because I was achieving great results in the form of book sales and high profit revenues, other authors began to ask me, *"How did you do it?" "Will you teach me?" or "Will you do the same thing for my book or for me?"* I was invited to speak at publishing and author events and before I knew it, I was being crowned the *Queen of Internet Marketing.*

I had not planned on the growth in this area of my business but I enjoyed teaching people about marketing so I embraced it. My passion for personal growth was still there, but a new passion— for helping others to market their books successfully—had grown so strong that it became the focus of my business.

As you look at your own passion, think about how your business might expand in a new direction. Might you teach others how you do what you do? Could you offer personalized services, work with a group of students, or even write a book based on your expertise? Think of all the many ways you could build upon your passion. My guess is you haven't begun to imagine them all!

#6: Sometimes Trying Things Leads to Greater Knowledge

As I said, once I'd generated large volume book sales for my own books, other authors started to flock to me for help marketing their own books. It didn't take me long to realize that I could teach these authors how to make their own books a best-seller *and* how to have a profitable experience at the same time. I realized that others could benefit from my own investment, and from what I had discovered through experience and a proven track record. My risks paid off (although sometimes they paid off even better than I imagined!). I discovered that I could make money teaching others what I now knew.

Was it part of my plan in the early days of setting up my business Dynamic Destinies, Inc., to teach authors how to make their books into best-sellers or to teach people how to make money marketing online? Heck no. But there was a demand, I knew I could effectively deliver on it, *and* I found that I loved helping other authors and loved teaching Internet marketing. I tried it; I loved it! Helping authors became a deep passion for me, and I decided to move into an area that not only fulfilled my desire to help others (specifically, authors), but to create another profitable revenue source for my business.

Trying something new often means taking a risk. You might lose a little money, or you might not achieve the results you'd hoped for given your investment of time. If you don't take risks, you may not discover an exciting new avenue for making a profit. Invest your time and money without risking more than you can afford, and pay close attention to the lessons you're learning. You might be very surprised at how your investment pays off.

#7: Make Sure You Do the Tummy Test

When I first began marketing my books on the Internet, and I was getting great results, I just assumed that every author must be marketing their books online. I was surprised to find out that they weren't. So, when authors started to ask me to show them, guide them, or actually do the online marketing work for them, I was genuinely surprised by their requests. Was this a service I wanted to provide to others? I knew I had to do the "tummy test."

What's the tummy test? It is simply consulting with your *inner knowing,* or listening to your *intuitive voice* when you ask yourself the question, "Is this what I really want to do and, is this in alignment with my purpose?" I was very clear that my purpose was "*to make a positive contribution to the lives of millions of others.*" Knowing that, and realizing that I had to be in alignment with that, made my decision easy (and quick).

If you don't know what your purpose is, doing the tummy test may actually help you discover it. If it just feels wrong to branch out in a certain direction, ask yourself why. What doesn't feel right when you imagine yourself taking this new path with your business? If you brush aside a gut feeling that a new venture isn't right for you, you will probably regret it. Slow down and take the tummy test. Even if you discover this change in your business plan isn't right for you at this time, you will come to know much more about what your purpose and values are.

#8: Know When to Say "That's Not for Me"

In the early days of running my business, when I offered soft skills training to corporations and government departments, I quickly realized that I wasn't doing what I loved. I discovered that as confident as I felt delivering the training, and much as I loved to teach, I find it difficult to keep up my own enthusiasm when my students are not excited about learning. Their employers had told my students that the training was mandatory therefore; they didn't come to me as "willing" students. I learned that my preference is to work with people who willingly come to my training and have a desire to apply what I'm teaching.

My insight was helpful for me because I realized I needed to shift gears and move away from the work that wasn't fulfilling into creating revenue, doing work that was fulfilling. I could change my style of presenting the material, but I could not change the fact that many of these students had absolutely no interest in doing anything more than "filling a seat" to please their boss.

You may find that while you might enjoy some aspect of your work, there is another aspect that you're simply never going to like and that you can't change. You may not like working with certain groups or types of people because of the nature of how you work. (Remember, you can never change other people, only approach them differently in the hope that their response will change). When you realize that you are not going to be happy with the situation as it is, and you can't change it, be willing to say, *"That's enough of that!"* Trust that other opportunities will present themselves.

#9: Keeping Your "Day Job" Isn't Such a Bad Idea

One of the first events I attended as a new author was a Book Marketing Conference in Los Angeles. I remember hearing one of the speakers say, "Don't quit your day job and pursue a career as an author." With loving intent, she wanted to instill in the minds of authors and business people the message that if you have a day job, and it is providing an income for you, keep the day job while you build your new business or career. It is much easier to remain calm and clear-headed in making business decisions when you're not worried about cash flow and finances. Allow yourself the cushion of time and money you need before making the leap to full-time Internet marketing and creation of your own products and services. Only you can know for sure what your comfort zone is, but make certain you give yourself plenty of breathing room.

One of my mentors taught me the following: When you set your business goals, expect that things will take much longer than anticipated. I recall hearing his words and sarcastically thinking at the time, *"Well, that's positive!"* Yet I learned that he was absolutely right. As you read further in this book, you will discover how to set and manage objectives, intentions, and goals *and* discover how to create a revenue model and analyze it before you even begin investing time, energy, or money.

CHAPTER 2

MONETIZE YOUR PASSION

Enthusiasm and persistence are both necessary ingredients to success. Your passion is the fuel to get you started and keep you going, but if you haven't created a revenue model for your business, you may end up struggling and creating undesired challenges.

I'll admit that when I wrote my first book I did not have a revenue model. I was under the ignorant assumption that if you write a great book the buyers will come, but that did not turn out to be my experience! At some level, I was expecting to make money from the sales of my book alone, but I quickly learned that this was not going to happen. I had to find a way to sell my books and generate profitable revenue by producing and marketing products and services that were needed in the marketplace. I needed to distinguish between the products and services that would build my credibility and my following but not necessarily turn a profit and those that would yield a strong financial return on my investment. The challenge was to strike a balance between the two so that I was both fostering my brand and generating needed revenue.

#10: There Has to Be a Need in the Marketplace for Your Product Right Now

I have worked with many experts and authors who get an idea in their head for a product or service to bring to the marketplace and then invest a ton of energy, time, and money into creating the product and making it available online, only to have it not sell. Lack of sales doesn't necessarily mean there isn't a need for your product or service in the marketplace, but it is possible. It is important to look honestly at whether your marketing campaign didn't appeal to your potential customers, or whether the number of potential customers for what you are selling is minimal.

During the recession, an expert that I am aware of created a product that would help people with investment strategies. He had a challenge selling his product because most people were concerned with simply staying afloat or keeping their homes; they weren't looking for investment strategies. He might have done better if he had released the product when the economy was booming or on the rise, not when things were at their worst and people did not have much cash to invest.

Before you bring your product or service to the marketplace, think about whether there is really a need for this product or service right now, before you invest the effort, time, and money in something that doesn't provide any return.

#11: You Have to Be Able to Deliver

Even though there may be a need for your product in the marketplace right now, it doesn't mean that anyone who can fog a mirror can deliver on it. When the social media craze began, folks who had no experience in business started to offer programs on "how to build a business" or "how to make money with social media" and yet they hadn't created success for themselves. I believe we have to earn the right to deliver on a product and service. Every single one of my products and services has come from my own experience and successes (and in some cases, failures or as I prefer to call them, "learning experiences").

I started teaching authors how to make money from their expertise and how to make their books best-sellers when I had created significant revenue from my own books *and* achieved numerous successes with online best-seller campaigns. I earned the right to teach what I knew from experience, not what I knew simply from observing others who had achieved success. That's why I knew I could deliver what I was promising. There was nothing "theoretical" about what I was teaching. I was telling people about proven techniques, so I knew the courses I was delivering were of great value.

#12: People Need to Be Willing to Pay for What You Are Selling

Everyone loves a freebee, but are people willing to pay your price for the products and services you are offering?

My clients were authors willing to invest in discovering how to make their books into best- sellers. Authors are very passionate about their message and the reason they write their book in the first place is because they want to get their work into the hands of readers.

When you start to do research online and take a look at what other people are offering in your area of expertise, you may find people offering similar products at a wide range of prices. Some may even offer them for free. What others are charging can offer you guidelines when you determine your pricing but more importantly, you need to determine what the value might be in the eyes of a customer. What do you believe people may be willing to pay for your product or service? And are you clearly communicating the value of the product or service by identifying the benefits to the customer? A customer always wants to know WIIFM (What is in it for me?) and it is up to you to make sure they are aware of the benefits and value. It is not enough to say, "I have made books into best-sellers using my marketing techniques, so take my course." You have to say, *"I have made books into best-sellers using my proven marketing techniques which I will share with you. At the end of the course, you will know how to make your book a best-seller."*

Take a close look at any copy that you create to promote your products and services. Scrutinize your Web site. Are you simply tooting your horn, or are you telling your customer what you can do for him or what your product or service will do for them?

#13: Set Your Revenue Objectives

Once you have established the products you are going to sell, you should create a revenue model around it. For example, when I released my book Your Destiny Switch, I had already created courses and mentoring services and adjunct products (audio downloads and CDs) to complement the messages in the book.

I recommend that you set your revenue objectives based on what you would like to generate and be sure to include the word "profitable" in your plan. I've seen some folks create great revenue-producing businesses and brag about them, but what they aren't sharing is the actual cost of doing business. If your business isn't producing a profit, it won't survive (unless you have unlimited funds to keep it going for an endless period of time).

Again, not everything you sell has to turn a profit. You can have a "loss leader" product or service that gets people in the door and excited about your brand and what you are offering. However, you must then convert those followers into customers who buy your profit-making products and services. If you are losing money on every sale, and not moving your profitable merchandise, you will not be in business for long!

#14: Create a Solid Profit-Generating, Revenue Producing Plan

There is an old axiom that goes like this: *"If you fail to plan, you plan to fail."* Is that true? Well, my personal belief is that you may succeed even if you don't have a plan per se but I do think that having a plan will accelerate and maximize your success.

When I start the calendar year, I establish a profit and revenue goal for the year. In order to achieve that goal, I establish the multiple projects I will execute. Each project has a deadline for completion as well as for launching, a metric (a measurement criteria) that will allow me to determine if my efforts are working or not, cost justification allowing me to evaluate the costs versus the profits, a list of the resources I will need to develop and market the product or service, the people who will support me in my creation and launch, and a list of weekly goals that I check off as I complete them. Each week, I work with an "Accomplishment List" where I detail all that I will accomplish during that week based on my projects lists. Every item on that page lines up with one of my projects and contributes toward my overall revenue goal. Having this goal plan puts me on track and keeps me there.

#15: Be Accountable to Your Plan

For several years now, I have had meetings three times a week with my mastermind buddy, Arielle Ford. Arielle and I connected several years ago when we were part of another mastermind group. We found that we were the ones from the mastermind group who consistently followed through with the commitment to check in with each other, present a challenge we were facing or a plan we wanted to carry out, and offer our feedback and suggestions. We decided it would serve us better if we simply worked together and created our own version of a mastermind group involving just us two and kept each other accountable. We called ourselves the *"mastermind duo"*.

On Monday morning, I e-mail Arielle my accomplishment list for the week. It starts with my regular opening statement: *"This week I will easily, harmoniously, and joyfully, for the good of all concerned, accomplish the following…"* and then I list my items. Arielle sends me her list back, using the same opening statement or a similar one. Even though Arielle and I are on the opposite sides of North America (she is in California and I'm in Ontario), and there is a time difference, we do not miss our meetings. We support each other, keep each other accountable, and are dedicated to our goals. You might set up a mastermind meeting in which each person reports on what he's accomplished for the week and what he intends to accomplish, and then you discuss what went well, and what needs to be done. It can be helpful to explore a tendency toward procrastination and have someone else gently point out to you that your time management skills could use improving. A good mastermind partner is always positive, enthusiastic, and yet honest about what you might improve upon.

#16: Be Flexible

One thing I've learned for sure is that you need to be flexible, especially if you are doing business on the Internet. As you are building your online business, stay flexible to the needs of the marketplace, your method of delivery, and your revenue forecasts.

The timing of your product may need to change if the market conditions aren't right. For example, if you are releasing a product that is perfect for gift giving, you don't want to launch it just after one gift giving season has ended and another one is still long off in the future. If you are late in creating it, you must still work with the buyers' mood at any given time.

Your product may need to be adjusted to reach the widest possible audience. One of my clients was frustrated to hear that his book, which was chock full of information, was too intimidating to interested buyers who wanted something simpler that would take less time to read. He discovered that he could sell the book to one group of people and also create an abbreviated version of it for the second group, which preferred a shorter, simpler product. If you receive constructive criticism about your product or service, be grateful for the feedback that can help you adjust what you are offering to maximize its sales potential.

#17: Some Prospects Are More Valuable Than Others

When I first began marketing on the Internet, I studied a number of successful online marketers' programs. One such expert explained that a good rule of thumb is that every prospect is worth $1 to you. The expert went on to explain that if you are driving 10 prospects to your Web site, and 10 percent of those prospects turn to customers who spend on average $10, that customer is worth $1.

This logic made sense to me, however, you could be driving prospects to your Web site all day long, but if you aren't selling them anything, or you are selling something but no one is buying, the prospects aren't worth anything! Having said that, you need to create a plan to drive prospects to your Web site and be ready to convert them to paying customers when they get there. Also, if you are driving prospects to your Web site and you are attempting to convert them to customers, but they aren't converting, it is time to reevaluate your marketing messages (see Chapter 5: Effective Copywriting).

#18: Don't Underestimate the Value of Your Established Customers

The value of an established customer is probably one of the most ignored revenue producing areas in any business. Most businesses focus the majority of their efforts on attracting new customers, when they could be better off focusing their efforts on selling more to their existing client base (assuming they have one of course). If someone has already purchased a product or service from you in the past, and you have provided him with value, isn't he a more likely prospect than someone who has not already had an excellent experience buying from you?

My friend John Assaraf, a successful businessman who teaches the principles of running a profitable business, taught me that the chances of your existing customers spending more money with you are far greater than you may think. He says that selling to your established clients is one of the most overlooked areas in most businesses and if business owners focused on it more, it would be more fruitful.

Of course, to sell to your previous customers, you must keep track of them. Give them an incentive to stay in contact with you. Send them an email asking for feedback on the product. Offer a free informative newsletter they can sign up for or ask them to sign up for your blog. Use social media to interact with them, as this will ensure that you know just where they are when you have something new to offer them.

Chapter 3

PUTTING THE PLAN INTO ACTION

To put your plan for Internet marketing into action, you must first establish your brand and your Internet presence. Otherwise, you may have a successful campaign but you won't build a loyal customer base. They may not remember where to find you again should your product leave them wanting more. You may have expertise in more than just the one area they are familiar with due to your product. Get them interested in you and your brand and all that you have to offer.

As I said, my first Web site was a static brochure on the web, which was helpful to some degree but it was not the best use of this valuable marketing tool. You can miss many opportunities to make money marketing on the Internet if you think short-term and focus on launching one product instead of setting the foundation for a booming business that will offer you many possibilities for building a larger client base and selling more products and services. Fortunately, today it is easier than ever to get your brand and your business up and running so that you can start creating and selling what your potential customers need and desire.

#19: Have a Clear Brand

A brand can be communicated in a few words. For example, part of my branding message is that *"I help authors make their books into best-sellers."* There is much more than I actually do but that is one of my branding messages. My sister Judy's business is called Hasmark Services and her brand includes "the **h**eart **a**nd **s**oul of **mark**eting" and she creates best-selling campaigns for authors. Sometimes people ask me what Judy and I do, and how our services differ. I explain, *"I help people learn how to fish, so they can eat for a lifetime while Judy does the fishing for them."* (Believe me, plenty of people would love to have someone do the "fishing" for them and they are happy to invest in that type of service!)

A brand needs to convey your style. If you are "all business," your brand should make that clear. If you offer a personal touch, be sure you communicate that. Be creative in coming up with your slogans, text, logo and graphics that will be associated with your brand but always keep your messaging congruent. Make sure your potential customers know right away the core of what you have to offer and be consistent with promoting your brand in all of your communications, and with your online presence.

#20: Be Clear on How You Want Your Web Site to Serve

Before you design your new Web site or redesign your old one, you need to determine how you want your site to serve you and others. Is it your desire to do business through your Web site (that is, do you want to sell products and services over the Internet)? Or is your site's purpose to give your customers more information about your brand and teach them where they can purchase what you are selling? (For example, if you want to do wholesale sales, you might prefer to speak to people over the phone and make it clear on your site that you do not do retail sales). Do you want to secure speaking engagements, get media attention, or build a prospect list? Do you want your site to serve many functions? Or, do you want to have several sites?

Whatever you desire, plan in advance the items you want to have on your Web site. One of the easiest things you can do to create a great Web site is to find some other sites that are accomplishing what you wish to accomplish and model your site after theirs.

#21: Know Your Target Audience

Being everything to everybody may not be your best strategy. Niche marketing can be an excellent way to generate profits. To be in a niche market, you must know your target audience and what you need to communicate to them, and how, in order to make a sale. A niche market for me is providing services to authors who write, publish or self publish and they want their book to be a best-selling book. Although my Internet marketing techniques have been successfully used by many outside of this niche (entrepreneurs, small business owners, experts, etc), it's easy for me to go back to my target audience to sell new products and services. Satisfied customers recommend my products to their peers, which is how I built such a strong client base of authors. I'm happy to have my customers do word-of-mouth advertising for me! And if they recommend me to people who have a different goal for using Internet marketing, that's great too, because I know I have products and services that will match their needs.

Entrepreneurial women tend to find their way to me as well because I'm a woman and I'm an entrepreneur. Sometimes you'll attract your audience to you without even planning on it (as I did with authors). Sometimes, if you think about whom would most benefit from your products and services, the target audience will suggest itself. One of my clients has a book that appeals to parents but also to teachers and professionals who work with children who have specific learning needs. You might think about whom besides "the usual suspects" would appreciate what you are selling. Who knows? You may find there's a larger target audience than the one you'd originally planned to reach!

#22: You Can Find the Perfect Web Person to Work With

I have personally been very blessed with finding and working with wonderful web people but I know there are many others who have not. They've felt ripped off because they spent a lot of time and money building or revamping their site only to end up with one that doesn't represent them or sell their product(s) and/or service(s) well. When you're first starting out, you might think there are not many professionals available to you, especially if you are on a budget. Think positively. You do not have to settle for someone who is difficult to work with, uncooperative, inflexible, or expensive. I certainly wouldn't work with someone like that.

The web designer I deal with currently is Colin Miller. He runs a business called One Graphic and you can find him at http://onegraphic.com The reason I rave about Colin and his service is that he's *great* at what he does but also, he is thorough, responsive, kind, and deeply caring. He is one of those people who delivers more than was promised. I know from talking to other clients that there are other professionals like Colin out there and they don't necessarily cost a fortune to work with. Ask around and listen to your instincts when choosing professionals. Trust that you can find the best people and you will.

#23: Maintain a Healthy Relationship with Your Web Designer

Mark Victor Hansen, who is a great mentor and friend of mine, always used to say, "Be nice to everyone" and I totally agree. I believe that in life and business, it's critical to be understanding, patient, and completely respectful with others. I apply this to working with web designers. I've watched web masters create their magic and I've created web pages and sites myself so I know web design work is truly time consuming. Plus, it is important to understand that your web person very likely has other customers who are expecting or demanding their services and they probably have deadlines. As important as it is to you to make changes to your Web site or fix what you see as flaws, be sure that your eagerness to get the job done immediately doesn't result in your web designer feeling pressured or disrespected.

My recommendation is to express your appreciation to your web person at every opportunity. Also, if you are not sure of your designer's workload, ask how long he thinks it will take to do the work you are requesting. If you have a specific date in mind, make your request respectfully and clearly. There are times when you may need your web person to go above and beyond the call of duty, but if he or she has had unpleasant experiences with you, your designer may not be too open to your requests.

#24: Fresh Content is Absolutely Critical

If you want people to return to your Web site, regularly post fresh content whether it is articles, blog entries, tweets, recommendations and links, contests, or something else. One of the reasons blog sites are popular is because the content is always fresh. Social media has taken off in part for the same reason. Many smart marketers are using these sites to build their platform and following because on social media they are providing fresh content. They can post something brief on social media and at the same time remind customers of the valuable information on their Web site. For example, when children are headed back to school, you can offer a valuable tip or two for making that transition easier on the whole family and post a link to the section on your Web site that has back-to-school tips. If there is an item in the news that relates to one of your services, post a comment on a social media site and link back to your services page on your Web site. Do not post the same comments or ideas over and over again, however. Your followers will become bored and stop checking in with you. Whether you are creating a short comment or a long blog post, keep it fresh.

#25: Be of Service

When you are an entrepreneur it may seem as if you don't work for anyone, but that couldn't be any further from the truth. You are working for someone, and hopefully, many people. Who are you working for? Your customers! No matter what business you're in, you are in business to be of service to others.

Perhaps you are selling a product, not a service. Even so, customer service matters. It can be inconvenient to explain to a confused customer exactly how to work with your product, or to immediately replace a part damaged in shipping or accidentally left out of the package. You may not want to have to ship orders the same or next day, but the better your customer service, the more satisfied your customers will be, and the more they will buy from you and spread the word about your business. Make the effort to be of service and you will be happy you did.

#26: You Are in the Problem-Solving Business

No matter what business you are in or what business you create, ultimately, you need to be in the problem-solving business if you are to be successful. What problems are you solving? I'm not talking about needs or wants or the difference between the two, or whether the problem is real or not, or urgent or not. What is an urgent need to one person may be a not-so-urgent desire for another. However, at some level, you need to be solving a problem for your customers. Perhaps your service or product saves them time and to them, time is of the essence so they value what you are selling. Perhaps what you offer helps them to feel good about themselves when their confidence is low, and solving the problem of feeling insecure when you want to feel bold is important to them. The authors who pay for my courses on how to make your book a best-seller using Internet marketing have a strong need to solve their problem of potentially minimal book sales and instead experience the joy of a best-seller. This very real benefit to my program has great value for them because it solves their problem.

"It's nice, but I don't really need it or want it" is not the reaction that will net you a profit! If you don't believe me, think about a time when you bought a product because its advertisement convinced you that it would solve a problem that, until now, you didn't know you had. Identify your customer's problem and tell her how your fantastic product or service will solve it.

#27: Opportunities Are Everywhere

Stop for one moment and look at the enormous opportunity that we have, for the first time in the history of this world, to reach potential customers *anywhere* around the globe instantly using the Internet. It truly is miraculous. The World Wide Web hasn't been around for very long but it has totally changed the human experience! Thirty percent of the people on earth are on the Internet. The number of users and the number of Web sites and pages continues to increase. Social media is expanding; one popular Web site, started six years ago, now has more than 500 million active users: That is 1 in 14 people in the entire world. What does all of this traffic on the Internet and on social media mean for you? *Opportunity.*

The opportunity to create a worldwide presence no matter who you are or where you are located is now possible. Translation software gets better all the time, expanding your abilities to communicate easily with people who speak a different language from yours. You can make sales to customers in countries that do not share your language. I remember marketing my very first book from the comfort of my home in a small town outside of Ottawa, Ontario, Canada. When people started buying my book from over 26 countries in the world I realized that the borders have come down. You can establish yourself as an expert almost overnight and create an unlimited revenue producing business within a very short period of time.

CHAPTER 4

BUILD IT AND THEY WILL COME

Remember Kevin Costner building a baseball field in the middle of a cornfield in *Field of Dreams?* He started with a vision of what he wanted to create and trusted that if he built the field, the people would come. I've found that starting with a vision and following through with action does work when you want to achieve a goal. However, when it comes to online marketing, you make it easier on yourself when you focus first on building your online presence and connections, and then create your product or services. This way, you don't get stuck sitting on inventory as I did when I wrote and created my first book and the copies from the printer filled my dining room.

Start with a Web site that serves as your web
presence, and then build upon that to create a
brand people remember, value, and recommend
to others. Make your site the place your customers come to regularly to shop and find out what's
new. Stay connected to them and you will find
you have built the foundation of a successful
business that can make the most of the invalua-
ble tool of Internet marketing.

#28: Drive People/Traffic to Your Site

Once your Web site is set up, you need to offer a
reason for people to come to your site. You
might give something away, share something of
value, sell valuable products and services—
whatever your intention, you must get visitors to
your site, also known as "driving traffic to your
site."

SEO, or search engine optimization, is one way
to make sure people find you because it will help
you rank higher in search engine listings of Web
sites. However, I have always found that the best
way to drive traffic that actually converts to sales
is to build visibility through additional means.
Don't focus so much on how many unique visitors you have as how many of your Web site's

visitors follow through with the action you want them to take: purchasing a product, offering you helpful information that you can offer others, signing up for a newsletter, or whatever it is.

#29: Have Clear Intentions Regarding What You Want Your Web Site Visitors to Do

Decide in advance what you want people to do when they come to your Web site. Do you want them to give you their e-mail address so that you can approach them later with a product? Do you want information from them that will help you create a product or service? Do you want them to interact with you so that your site serves as a gathering spot where people can feel heard? Do you want them to buy something you have for sale?

Your Web site design and text should make it clear what you want visitors to do. Make your sign-up box for your newsletter prominent. Put the clear expectation "Join now! Click here!" underneath an image of the product you are selling or the summary text spelling out your services. Video is another popular method to communicate what you want your visitor to do. Look at other successful Web sites to see how they have made clear to their visitors what they want them to do. Do they repeat a sign-up box on every page? Do they have a page devoted to the media so that journalists and reporters can quickly access their company's biography, press releases, and downloadable high-resolution photographs?

Although your Web site will change over time as you update and expand upon it, always be sure that your visitors will instantly and easily see what your expectations of them are.

#30: Give Something Away for Free

When you give something away for free people feel they have gotten a bargain when they receive something of value that they don't have to pay for. Freebees create goodwill and excitement. They can inspire customers to come back for more and to spread the word about your products and services to others because they are so excited about what you gave them for free.

You can give away free information in the form of audio, video, or text. You might create a free eBook or eCourse that you offer customers, perhaps in exchange for signing up for your monthly newsletter for offering you their e-mail address. You might offer a lot of valuable information on your site, such as checklists and articles. Blogging is another way to give away free information and you can ask people to subscribe to your free blog.

You can give away a physical product for free. When a customer orders a product, slip something in the envelope that will give them a nice surprise. There have been times when I've placed a free copy of my double-CD program called *Turn Fear into Faith* in the box when people ordered the six-CD program called *Magnet for Money Platinum Edition.* The customers weren't expecting the extra bonus in their package, but they were pleasantly surprised.

While you do not want to give away all that you know for free, it's interesting to see that when you are generous and offer people information that's valuable for no cost, they will often turn around and buy an extended version or a more detailed version which could include some of the same information in another larger, more complete product. Freebees create goodwill that often leads to revenue.

#31: If You Want Visitors to Do Something, Tell Them

If you want your Web site visitors to "buy your product" or "sign up for your newsletter" or "enter your e-mail address" it is up to you to tell them so. Be very clear on the instructions and make it as easy as possible for people to take action. If you want them to buy your product, you might feature a big picture of it on every page with a "Sign up now!" link underneath it. If you want them to sign up for your newsletter, don't just ask them once. Make sure they have the opportunity to do so on the home page and on other pages as well. Make it clear what benefits they will receive for performing an action and make it easy for them to commit to doing what you ask of them.

When I'm making a purchase online I find it challenging to have to hunt and navigate through a Web site to find what I'm looking for. Have a quality Web site design so that using your site doesn't confuse and frustrate visitors. Bring me to the page I want quickly and easily and I'll be more likely to continue through checkout without throwing up my hands and abandoning the shopping cart. Place icons where I would expect to find them. Shopping cart buttons are often placed in the top right hand corner on most popular sites. When people are shopping they know to look for their shopping cart when it is time to checkout. If the shopping cart button isn't in the top right hand corner and it is hard to find, you could be losing sales. Make pull-down menus obvious. Don't get so creative with your design that I am not sure where I am on the site or how I got there! I've landed on pages within a Web site and found myself lost and didn't know how to get back to where I started (the menus were different on each page). Help me to remember why I'm here visiting your site and what benefits I will find here. Then show me where to click so I don't leave and look for another, easier-to-navigate site.

#32: Upsell and Suggestive Sell

Your potential customer may come to your Web site to download a free eBook or sign up for your free eCourse or newsletter, but while he is there, use the opportunity to upsell and suggestive sell products and services you may make a profit on. Upselling refers to enticing customers into buying a second product/service that costs more than the one they were first interested in (although they may buy that one as well). Suggestive sell-ing refers to reminding the customer of other products they might enjoy as well, which are in the same price range or cost less. An example of suggestive selling would be the following – once the prospect has clicked on a product, a message would appear saying "customers who bought this product also bought these". This encourages ad-ditional sales, therefore, the total sale amount could be significantly larger than if they hadn't received the suggestion.

If the customer feels your original product is a terrific bargain, he is more likely to respond to your upselling or suggestive selling. A returning customer, who knows how great your products are, might spend more money this time on a higher-priced product or service. Many of my teleseminar clients come back to me for one-to-one coaching.

A new customer might feel that since one of your products is obviously quite a bargain or simply of interest to him, he may try another one. You might even offer a special for those who buy in quantity or who are willing to add a second product or service on to their offer. Your pricing can serve to suggestive sell, too: "For a limited time only, these products are $15 each or three for $35). Or, orders over $25 receive shipping for free.

#33: *Always* Focus on Customer Service

Many years ago I saw a poster with a photo of an old-fashioned, rotary dial telephone covered in cobwebs. Underneath was written: "If we don't take care of the customers maybe they'll stop bugging us." As humorous as this poster may have been, it delivered a powerful message. You cannot ignore your customers or prospective customers, no matter how busy you get.

Many times when I respond to general inquiries from my Web site, and I do so in a timely manner, people are surprised. Sometimes they'll ask, "Is this really Peggy, or an assistant?" They respond with disbelief when I tell them it's me. Could Peggy possibly be responding to e-mails that go to her general mailbox? Yes, of course I'm going to respond to e-mails. My business includes one full-time employee: me. When I require the services of other individuals, I hire them on an hourly basis or project/service basis. I have a number of people who help me with many aspects of my business, and each one of them is readily available.

If you delegate customer service to someone who is assisting you in your business, be sure you make clear your expectations about serving customers. Every person who answers the phone, writes copy for you, or responds to inquiries from customers needs to be customer service focused.

#34: Send a Clear Message about What Problems You Can Solve for the Customer

As you read earlier in this book, you are in the problem-solving business. You can never assume that people visiting your Web site will know what problems you can solve for them or the reason why *you* are the ideal problem solver. You have to spell it out for them.

Some visitors to your site will be vague about their problem. They may not know exactly what they are looking for. Offer the possibilities to them in clear language so that they can say, *"Yes, I have that problem! And I'd really like to solve it."* Then tell them how you can help them do so.

One of the problems that I solve is to how to create a book from your ideas, sell a book once it has been written and produce and create a profitable business from it. When I started out with my first self-published book, I had 3,000 copies sitting in my dining room. One problem I had was an inventory that needed to be sold so I could get my valuable information to people who could use it—and so I could use my dining room again! The other problem I had was that I needed to generate some revenue to offset some of my expenses. As it turned out after I started marketing online, not only did I clear out my inventory, but my revenues turned out to be very profitable. Now I help authors to solve their problem of having books they don't know how to sell and wanting to make money off selling those books. I am clear with the authors I work with that writing a book is wonderful, but if you write a book you want the public to embrace, and you invest money in its production, you now have two problems I can solve: the need to sell books and the need to make a profit.

#35: Be Attentive to Your Online Image

Whether you are posting articles, sharing quotations or videos, developing a presence on social media or on a blog, sending out a regular news-letter, or offering information on a Web site, everything you put on line is a representation of you and your brand or business! If you want people to think of you as a professional, be pro-fessional. If you want people to think of you as someone having integrity, demonstrate integrity. If you want people to believe you have some-thing of value, share content that is valuable. Be true to your vision of your brand and business and make sure it is reflected in your copy and any visual images you use to represent your business.

You can use privacy settings on social media to limit the personal information clients and poten-tial clients can access, but do share something of yourself in order to make a personal connection. I've noticed that when I post a photo about my son or my family, or something about my dog-gies, the people I'm connected with on the social media sites respond favorably. As a matter of fact, some folks have said that it helps show that I'm "real" and it seems to create a greater bond with them. You might post a link to a dog rescue site you support, a funny but noncontroversial video that reflects your sense of humor, or your reaction to a wonderful concert that you enjoyed over the weekend. Definitely keep personal information such as your full date of birth, your mother's maiden name, and so on, off any of your social media sites. (Think about the security questions sites ask for these days; do you really want people knowing the city you were born in or your high school mascot?)

Make sure your graphics on your Web site and your products are appropriate for your business and your brand. One client of mine had a site that featured a lot of pink, a color she liked but which didn't convey "business professional" to her clients. Another client needed to add more images to his site to convey that he offered "friendly" and "personal" service. Pay attention to the feel of the graphics and the tone of the text when you visit others' sites or look at their product packaging.

If you use a photo or image of yourself in marketing, such as a video welcoming visitors to your site, be sure that it conveys your professionalism as well as the feel of your brand. If you are selling something that is "natural" and "simple," you might use an image of yourself outdoors. Make sure that the experience your customer has when he goes to your Web sites, looks at your product packages, and reads your blog and social media posts is consistent.

#36: People Don't Care How Much You Know Until They Know How Much You Care

You can be an encyclopedia of information, but people will care more about how much you care than they do about how much you know. You can demonstrate that you care by the way you share your information. Don't hoard your information or offer it so freely that you give everything away. Both actions are rooted in fear, whether it's a fear of being taken advantage of or a fear of not being liked. Be confident and generous. Listen to others and respond. If there is a situation whereby you personally can't solve someone's challenge, offer them a resource or a link to offer help to find someone who can.

Tell people you care and show it by offering them thoughtful and helpful advice. If your client is feeling unsure of whether he can use your services at this time, help him talk through what he needs right now. He may need to go off and accomplish another task before coming back to you, but he will remember whom you are and how helpful you were to him. He may even send another customer your way before he is able to come back to you himself.

#37: Deliver Phenomenal Service and People Will Talk (Under Promise and Over Deliver)

As you develop your product and/or service, find a way to provide exceptional value. Make it well worth the price you are asking by digging a little bit deeper to discover that extra thing that folks will respond to by saying, "With that as part of the deal, I can't resist it. It's too good a value to pass up." People will not only purchase what you are selling, but will tell others what a great deal they got and create a Viral Explosion (that is, their word-of-mouth praise and recommendations will fly through the Internet and reach the eyes and ears of many potential customers for you).

One gentleman I know promises a four- to five-page written report for his customers for a fixed cost. He regularly adds another couple of pages of extra advice, insight, and information. When they see how much he has over delivered, his customers are thrilled. I have been known to stay on the phone after a teleseminar is over and offer extra advice and inspiration beyond what I promised to my attendees. I want them to leave feeling not just satisfied but excited to know that I genuinely care about them and I give more than expected.

CHAPTER 5

EFFECTIVE COPYWRITING

Have you ever heard the expression, "You get one chance to make a first impression?" When you are selling a product or service on the Internet, you have one chance to make a first impression on your potential customer. If you have put effort into getting people to your site, sales page or landing page, then you want to have effective copywriting that will turn the majority of your prospects into customers.

Be sure to communicate all of your messages with the highest of integrity. Yes, you can use copywriting to make yourself sound impressive, but don't create a false persona. Make sure your copy is true to yourself, your brand, and your business. Otherwise, you are only setting your-self and your customers up for disappointment. Also there are FTC (Federal Trade Commission) guidelines you need to adhere to (see the Re-sources section for a link to these guidelines).

You may wish to approach this area of exper-tise—copywriting—by learning how to write effective copy for yourself. The skill of writing sales copy is something that will serve you for-ever. However, you may still wish to hire a pro-fessional copywriter to ensure that you have the most compelling text possible.

You may have said these words yourself:

> *I am an author so I should be able to write my own sales copy.*

> *I am in the business of marketing so creat-ing a landing page is no big deal.*

Ah, if only these statements were true, 100 per-cent of the time! How humbling is that I am both an author and a marketer and I still seek outside collaborative help when it comes to creating a stellar landing page. I do it because I know how important it is to create a page that accomplishes the desired outcome: Sales!

You have a lot riding on a good sales page. You have already invested time and money to produce a product or deliver a service. Now, it's time to generate copy that will attract business.

#38: You Have to Grab People's Attention

Because I have learned copyrighting and I know what a valuable skill it is, I teach copywriting in my programs. I always emphasize to my students the importance of the subject line in an e-mail and the importance of headings and subheadings on your web pages and sales pages (also known as landing pages—these are one-page Web sites that serve to sell your products and services). You have to grab people's attention right away.

The reason some people have created an enormous following on blogs or social media sites is because they are really good at communicating a short message that grabs people's attention and causes them to want to know more. Everyone is busy and the Internet is full of distractions, from instant messages to active social media sites, and blogs where lots of action is happening. You have to engage people emotionally and intellectually, instantly, with a clear message that conveys a sense of urgency and excitement.

Grabbing people's attention is the starting point and an important element but it isn't everything. It's like the chocolate in a chocolate cake recipe. You have to combine it with other elements as well: Every single part of the copy you incorporate into e-mail, sales pages, your Web site, and social media is critical, too. Yet your customers won't get to see the rest of your communication if you don't get their attention right away. Take your time to generate, or have generated for you, the very best possible headers and subject lines for your communications to potential customers.

#39: Identify for Your Customers the Problem that You Can Solve for Them

People don't want to be sold to but they do want to buy. Your copy must clearly outline the problem the buyer is going to have solved by purchasing your product or service. It's not enough to sell them on what a dedicated professional you are, how many people you have served in the past, or how long you have been in business. You want your customer to feel a sense of urgency and excitement about having the chance to purchase a quality product or service from you that will solve a very real problem for them. Otherwise, their response will be, *"That sounds nice. I'll think about that later."* They'll move on to something else and forget all about your offer.

Some potential customers will be clear on what their problem is, but not all. You may need to point it out to them. They may also have a problem that doesn't feel urgent or important to them right now. In your copy, you can sell them on the urgency and importance of solving their dilemma. You do this by connecting to their emotions. Make them feel the need to solve their problem right now so that they are inspired to buy from you.

As you appeal to their emotions, you may find yourself wanting to appeal to people's fears and insecurities. That approach can be effective—after all how many cosmetics and sports cars have sold to people desiring to be more attractive? However, it's important to always communicate with a tone of compassion and understanding when appealing to people's emotions. Make sure your copy meets those criteria.

#40: Explain Why Other Solutions Haven't Worked or Don't Work and How Your Solution Has and Will

If you have someone interested in what you have to offer, they may have tried other solutions before. They may have invested in other people's products and/or services and been disappointed. Acknowledge their skepticism and the frustration they've experienced. Then assure them that your solution is different, that it is proven (or based on proven techniques or research) and that it will work.

You will often see this method of explaining what hasn't worked in the past, and why this new solution will, used to market weight loss programs. Buyers are looking for solutions. The marketing copy may reveal how this particular system is revolutionary and has solved the underlying problems that other programs don't deliver on. At the end of the day, your potential customers need to feel confident that you and your product will solve the problem they have, and will solve it once and for all.

#41: Offer the Solution and Be Specific

All prospects are tuning in to their favorite radio station, WII-FM. This stands for What's In It For Me? Every single prospect needs that question answered. What *is* in it for him or her? If you don't answer the question, your potential customer will be gone.

If your copy clearly communicates that you have the solution to that prospect's problem, and that you're certain they'll get the results they desire, *and* you back up your product with a 100 percent money-back guarantee, this gives your prospects the confidence to say "yes" to your offer.

Spell out exactly what the solution will be. Offer "before and after" examples if you can. You might show figures that illustrate dramatic results others achieved by using your product or service. I have seen landing pages that feature scanned checks (with the banking numbers removed) written to the person who is selling a program for making money. When your client sees what others achieved using your product or services, he or she will begin to feel some confidence in achieving similar results.

#42: Have Social Proof that Validates and Confirms Your Claims

Have others given you positive feedback for you, your product, or your service? If so, you may have a testimonial (also known as "social proof") that you can use for your copy on your special offer page (also known as "web page" or "landing page" or "sales page").

If you have a brand new product and service, you may want to give it away to others on a trial basis in order to generate some testimonials. If you don't have time to wait for others to try your product and provide you with feedback, you may want to get some character references who validate who you are and what you are able to achieve for your clients. For instance, if you are an expert in a particular field or genre, and you have helped people by providing quality services and products in the past, ask them to allow you to post a testimonial from them that will inspire confidence in your prospective clients. Often you will see a new book released by an author and instead of getting a massive number of new testimonials they will use some endorsements for the previous book or for that person's writing. "Character" references may include endorsements from well-known people who have endorsed that person's other work or books.

For the most part, people think of testimonials as icing on the cake of a good client experience. But don't underestimate your clients' ability to sell others on your credibility and expertise. Let's face it: Unless someone recommends your services, potential clients may be reluctant to trust you with their money. To earn that trust, you have to show them that you have a good track record and that your products and services have produced tangible results for people.

You can ask for testimonials from other experts in your field (who already have established their credibility). Once you do have a customer base, and you start to receive e-mails from clients extending their gratitude and appreciation for you and your products/services, ask the client if you can use their words as a testimonial. I'm always receiving e-mails from clients praising me for how I have helped them achieve their goals, and I keep this correspondence in a "feel good" folder on my computer. When a client sends me a nice comment, I'll immediately thank them, and ask them if they would mind if I use their testimonial in promotion.

You can use testimonials on your Web site, inside your emails, on social media, on all of your promotional pieces such as brochures. They really do make a positive difference. And when your customers praise you, ask them to please pass along the word to others who might benefit from your services and products.

#43: Reward Your Customers for Taking Immediate Action

People are busy and distracted. You don't want a prospective customer to put off buying from you until some indefinite time in the future. It is too easy to lose that customer. Make the sale and seal the deal by rewarding your customer for taking immediate action.

Having bonus gifts and extra goodies for anyone who buys now, without delay, is a great way to get people to make an immediate purchasing decision. You may also offer a discount for buyers making an early decision, such as "If you sign up before Friday, you'll save $100." Make yours a limited time offer. And make sure your prospect understands that if he hesitates, the offer may disappear, but if he buys now, he will receive an extra reward. The carrot (the reward) and the stick (the possibility that he may miss out on a terrific opportunity) combined have sold many products and services.

#44: Tell Your Customers What You Want Them to Do, and Remind Them More Than Once

Landing/sales pages often contain a great deal of copy. Your page should be jam packed with information about your product or service and its benefits. At the same time, it should offer many opportunities for the visitor to stop and "buy now" or "sign up now."

Never assume that a prospective client knows what you want him to do or that he will follow through on his intention to purchase without plenty of reminders from you. Purchase instructions need to be clearly communicated and blatantly obvious on a sales page and they need to be repeated in multiple places. People make decisions in different time frames. You can attempt to sell me something and, if I think it's of value to me and a good price, I'm probably going to buy after reading one or two paragraphs. I will be looking for a purchase button or buying instructions right away. However, if you try to sell my husband something, you had better be ready with some cold hard facts, and believe me, he'll read *all* of the copy before he makes a buying decision. He may see a half dozen "Hurry! Buy now!" buttons and will ignore them all, but when he gets to the bottom of the page he will be looking for the purchase instructions there. Make it easy for customers like him and me to purchase right at the moment when they make the decision. The more scrolling they have to do, the more likely you are to lose them.

#45: Answer All Potential Questions

One of the easiest ways you can create great copy is to anticipate the questions your prospect would be asking and make sure all of those questions are answered in your copy. For example, your prospects may be asking:

- Who is this person behind the product or service?
- Why should I buy from this person?
- Will their solution work for me? What if it doesn't?
- Who else has used it/followed them/bought from them?

- Can anyone else validate this person/the product?
- What will this product or service do for me?
- How quickly will it work?
- What is it and what format/form is it delivered in?
- Is there anything else I need to do or know before I buy?
- Why is this particular product or service finally going to solve my problem when other products and services haven't?
- What do I have to do now (if I want it)?

Make a list of the questions prospects may be asking themselves as they consider you, your product, and/or your service. Be certain that your copy is answering every single question.

#46: Copy Has To Be Convincing and Compelling

Regardless of how long or short it is, regardless of how it is delivered (in an e-mail, on a landing or sales page, on your Web site, on a social media site, or wherever it appears), *all* of your copy needs to be convincing and compelling. If people aren't sold on your offer, they will go away and may never be back. As they say, "Ladies and Gentleman, Elvis has left the building."

How do you make your copy convincing and compelling? There are many rules and tips to follow. Even the most talented writer may be a bit overwhelmed by the challenge of creating the very best copy. An investment in hiring a professional copywriter may pay off very well. If you are not planning to hire a copywriter to do the work for you, seek out a mentor to guide you in this particular type of writing. Because writing a great sales landing page is an essential element of successful product launch, I have included copy-writing techniques in my Online to Riches program (http://destinies.com/rich). Don't let this one piece of the puzzle stop you from sharing your talents, products, and services with the world.

CHAPTER 6

CREATING ONGOING REVENUE STREAMS

Earlier in this book, I mentioned the importance of creating a revenue model for your business. Since the Internet is like a store that remains open 24 hours a day and 7 days a week, with shoppers from all over the world lining up, you have an opportunity to create ongoing revenue streams.

You may find, as I did, that your lineup of products might change from time to time. Some products will never have an expiration date and will be perennial sellers while others will be popular for a period of time and then their sales will fade. Let's look at how you can create a constant revenue stream that provides you with income no matter where you are (even on a beach in the Caribbean!) and no matter whether you are actively working on your business when the sale is made, or not.

A few years ago, my husband, Denis, and I were on our honeymoon in Hawaii, and although I obviously didn't work while we were there, I did have my Blackberry with me. Whenever I checked it, I could see that orders continued to come in even though I was away from the office for a period of time. I've gone to sleep at night and woke up the next morning having generated revenue, and as they say, "That's making money in your sleep." You, too, can make money while you are doing something else if you create ongoing revenue streams through effective Internet marketing.

#47: Start with a Great Product

As you think about any particular product or service you might offer for sale, ask yourself these three questions:

1. Where is there a need in the marketplace that a product or service of mine might address?

2. Can I fulfill that need and does it line up with my brand?
3. Would people be willing to pay for my product or service?

If the answer is "yes, yes, and yes!" you have a winner.

If you see a need in the marketplace, but you can't fulfil it, simply look for another need. It doesn't matter if everyone is buying widgets these days because they are the "hot" item to own if you have no interest or expertise in creating or marketing widgets. Find a niche that matches up with your brand and identify a need you can fill.

Here are some types of products you can create:

- Audio recordings (downloadable or on a CD or flash drive)
- Tool kit or Owner's Manual that takes the reader deeper into your content
- Home study course or workbook
- Instructional teleseminars with related Power Point
- Interview recordings (audio or video) of people who were your mentors, or people

who have benefited from your work, or who are in a similar genre.

#48: Don't Just Offer a Product or Service, Offer a Lineup of Products and Services

Remember how I said your satisfied customers will want to come back for more? The question is, will you have further products and services to offer them? I hope so because you can generate a lot of revenue by offering a line-up that meets the needs of your various customers.

One way to create a line-up of products or services is through repurposing material you already have. I've created products based on audio recordings from teleseminars I've done. I have expanded on the advice I gave in my teleseminars and written books on those topics.

Some people will want personalized services while others would prefer to work with you as part of a group. Some will want an audio version of your information while some would prefer to see a visual rendering, such as a Power Point presentation or a video—and they might even wish to have the material in the form of a book. You can find many different ways to reach many different audiences using the same or similar material to that which you created previously.

#49: Have Your Products Available 24/7

On my own Web site, I sell audio CD products, downloadable products, and an entire course preloaded onto a flash drive. These products are available for purchase 24 hours a day 7 days a week. Basically, it is like having your own store open 24/7 although you don't need to have staff on hand to process the payments. Software will do that for you.

Set up your products to be purchased through an online shopping cart or an online merchant/ payment service. If your plan is to partner up with affiliates to have them promote your products, and share in the revenue, you will need shopping cart software or a payment method that can track each individual affiliate's sales. You will learn more about partnering in the next chapter.

Although your customers will probably not expect instant shipping of tangible items such as CDs and flash drives, they will expect prompt shipments using services that allow them to track their packages. If you create these types of products, set yourself up for shipping them out promptly.

#50: Set Boundaries for Yourself

If you offer services to people, *you* don't have to be available 24/7. Set boundaries for yourself and communicate them clearly. It still surprises me when I get a follow up e-mail on a Monday morning asking me to reply from their original message sent Friday afternoon or even Saturday. Really? One of the strategies Tim Ferris talks about in *The 4-Hour Work Week* is to let people know when you are working and when you are out of reach. You can create an auto-responder to e-mails saying you are in the middle of a project and will check e-mail once a day, twice a day, etc. You can also post a status update on your social networking sites that you do not have access to e-mail during a particular day (without telling them that you are vacationing in Jamaica and your house is empty, which might attract burglars!) A nicely worded Do Not Disturb message will be well-received and respected.

#51: One Product or Service Can Lead to Developing Other Products and Services

A number of years ago I began to deliver a workshop called Propensity for Prosperity. It was evident that many people have a need to learn techniques for attracting the abundance they deserve. I delivered this workshop in a hotel in downtown Ottawa and afterward, I asked myself, "Is there any way that next time, people from all around the world could attend?"

That question led me to create a program I could offer online. I changed the name to the Magnet for Money Intensive Program and developed it as an 8-week course to be delivered over the phone and the Internet with weekly lessons, open Q & A time with me, and downloadable support materials in the format of Word and Adobe .pdf documents. I successfully marketed it to people on my e-mail list as well as to people on affiliates' e-mail lists and filled the class with students from all over the globe.

If you provide services to people locally, don't underestimate your ability to develop services or products to people who can't meet with you in person. Think about how someone many miles away who has phone and Internet access might be able to benefit from your knowledge and advice. What products and services might you create for that person?

Remember what I said about repurposing your material to create new products? My Magnet for Money online program created a demand for the material, so I produced a six-CD physical product that I could sell from my Web site and at live events. This audio program, appropriately named the Magnet for Money Platinum Edition, is still a very hot seller at my Web site, destinies.com

#52: You Can Create and Sell a Product Very Quickly

How quickly can you create a product and service and begin to market it online? Depending on how well your information is already organized and your own skill set as far as putting together programs, you could create a new program, prepare the marketing copy, and begin to market it in as little as 30 days.

The second Internet marketing campaign that I ever did came as a result of people buying my first book, *On Being...The Creator of Your Destiny*. Once people started to read my book and apply its principles, they were hungry for more. I would receive e-mails from readers asking me, "When are you doing a seminar in my city?" I was a single mother at the time and had no desire to travel all over the world delivering seminars. So, I asked myself, "How can I serve others from the comfort of my home?" and I decided by way of an "e" course (an electronic course that is delivered solely over the Internet). I created the name, The 8 Proven Secrets to SMART Success and designed the outline. I created a sales page with promotional copy, partnered up with some other Web site owners, and began to market the program within 30 days. One week after I sold the program, I began to deliver the lessons (one week at a time). I built the program as I was delivering it, which meant I did not have to have the entire program completed before I started to market it.

If you'd like to sell a product based on your expertise, think about how quickly you could pull your information together. Sketch out the steps you will have to take to market it, and plan the amount of time you will need. You might be very surprised at what you discover because it is definitely possible to create and sell a product in a matter of weeks.

#53: Don't Get Stuck in the Details

As entrepreneurs, we are talented when it comes to coming up with ideas and concepts, but we can get paralyzed when it comes to figuring out all of the details of developing them. We think we need to be experts at everything, or even worse, we think we have to figure everything out on our own.

I had a mentoring client who wanted to promote a DVD he created. He was at the beginning stages of planning his launch so he sought me out for guidance. He was overwhelmed with all the choices and tasks before him: what to put on his Web site, how to launch it, how to find partners, how to determine his pricing models, etc.

The best question he asked me was, "You have done this before, so, what did you do that was successful and how can I adapt it to my launch?" I have products, I have a production room in my house, and I have researched packaging and shipping options. I went through all of his options with him to help him tailor my successful strategies to his specific needs. Simply duplicating what I did may not work for everyone but I am certainly experienced enough to help people create their own path based on the principles of successful Internet marketing that I have learned through marketing my own products and services.

When I started out, I did not know everything and I certainly did not try to figure it all out on my own. Start by learning the basics of successful Internet marketing and doing research online. You could hire me, or invest in one of my Internet marketing products or courses. You have made a smart choice by picking up this book. It would be an even wiser decision to implement these ideas as well. Reach out to mentors and teachers who have taken the path before you and ask them for their best advice, as well as for answers to specific questions you have. I have always found that people are eager to help when approached with respect or even more eager when you hire them ☺

#54: Quality Must Be a Priority

When you release a product into the world, people will get an impression of you and the level of quality you have to offer them. People are not easily fooled these days. If you want people to think your products are of high quality, you need to make sure that they are.

When I self-published my books, I specifically chose quality paper, quality book covers, and professional editors, typesetters, designers, and printers to work with. It was important to me that people received a product that they could feel provided value for their money. In fact, when I have created free products for giveaways, I've ensured that they were well-produced also. If my name is on it, if my brand is associated with it, I want it to represent my high standards.

Your services need to be of the highest quality you can offer. Do your very best and charge an appropriate price for your high quality work.

#55: People Always Want More

When we listen to great speakers or authors, and we like their message, we buy their books. When we really connect with the content and style of their writing, we want more. We look for other books they have written or products they've created. We sign up for their newsletters, follow them on social media, and may even pay to get a personal consultation with them.

Early in my career as an author, when I would receive an e-mail from a reader wanting more—asking me if I had any other products—I was actually surprised. I wondered why would they want or need more when they had all of this great content available to them in my book. I had to stop and think, what else do I have to offer or what additional formats could I deliver them in? When I asked myself that question, I realized I did have more for them. I began creating products in earnest and expanding the services I offered.

Even if you feel you have put everything you know into one information-based product, such as a course or a book, you need to be ready to respond to the customer demands for other products. Think about different spins on your material, whether it is creating a beginner's guide, or a product that addresses special circumstances that you didn't cover in great detail in your previous product. Let your imagination work for you!

#56: Build a List of Followers by Giving Them Something for Free

One of the best things you can do for your online business is to build a database of prospective customers (and of course, paying customers, too). You can accomplish this by giving away valuable free gifts.

Create some downloadable free gifts and direct people to a page on your Web site where they can download free extra gifts such as:

- Special tip sheets
- Quizzes that help them better understand their problem and why you have the solution
- Posters that highlight the main lessons you teach people
- Mini-workbooks with exercises you've created, including those you have demonstrated on stage or in your book
- Weekly, monthly, or quarterly newsletters with new updates and features
- Daily tips, quotations, or words of wisdom
- Audio files of recorded interviews or teleseminars

- Transcripts from interviews or teleseminars
- User guides with templates for putting your strategies into action
- Analysis tools

#57: Maintain a Balance between Your Work and Your Personal Life

Weekends used to be just that: the end of your week. They were also the end of your work (at least, for a couple of days!), a time when you could enjoy some well-deserved rest and relaxation. As a solo-preneur or entrepreneur, I find it much harder to have established work days and hours than when I was working for a company. I have the luxury of working from my own home but that also blurs the line between work and personal life. Even if I close the office door and completely turn off my computer I still have the sense that e-mails, orders, questions and new ideas are just behind the door, waiting for me. I know there is more that can be done to build my business, generate revenue, and serve my clients. It is hard for me to stop and say "Enough for now!"

The great news is we can be connected to our business associates 24/7—yea! The challenge is to create the balance that allows you to live your life, and not just have a career. If you look at the world today and the way it was 20 years ago, even if you had your own business back then you could still leave your work and be disconnected. Knowing that, you have to set boundaries not just for your clients but for yourself. On my Web site I list the hours for phone calls in an attempt to create clear business hours and availability for my clients. I do not offer 24/7 service and I do what I can to remind people there are boundaries for my business. At the same time, I catch myself working extra hours and then, before I leave my office, I am tempted to check my e-mails to see if anyone was trying to get a hold of me.

I love my work but I don't make it my life. Too often, I see people in restaurants who have their phone on the table while they are having dinner with friends and family. As difficult as it is to schedule time together, cherish the connection and the conversation and leave the phone alone. That e-mail can wait, the text message is not an emergency, and the phone call is better enjoyed when the other party has your full attention.

CHAPTER 7

PARTNERING FOR SUCCESS

Although it's helpful to have a large database or a presence online to get started marketing on the Internet, it is not necessary. Find people who do have them and ask if they can help you market your product or services. Be honest with them about the difference you can make in people's lives, help them understand the benefit they will receive and explain how they can help you reach your target audience.

So why would complete strangers become your partners? These simple answers may surprise you:

1. They may simply want to help you. You might be surprised at how many truly

nice and generous people are interested in supporting you. Too often, people minimize the need for support in successful marketing. Don't underestimate the universe. It is a kind and supportive place!

2. If you have something of value that will help their customers, they may want to make their list aware of it and support you at the same time.

3. If you have an affiliate opportunity for revenue sharing, you would be offering them an opportunity to make money. It is easy for them to assist you because you'll create the product, write the copy, set up the Web site, fill the orders, *and* write the e-mail that they will send out to their people.

4. They may have an easy downloadable product that you can offer as a bonus gift which not only gives them exposure to your list, but to the lists of all of your other partners.

With the potential to reach millions of people, doesn't it make sense to invest the time talking (or writing) to strangers? That is how easy it is to create success quickly and profitably.

#58: You Can Build an E-Mail List of Followers by Working with Partners

Most people started marketing on the Internet without a list. They chose to partner with other folks, also known as list owners. These list owners were willing to promote the other person's product or services (or freebee) to their subscriber base. Note that a list owner doesn't have to give you his list to help you out. In fact, I don't recommend that. Have *him* send an e-mail to his subscribers recommending your product or service. You will provide him with this email naturally. His subscribers trust him not to sell or give away their e-mail addresses and both of you should honor that.

When I did my very first Internet campaign to sell a book I had written, it generated tens of thousands of dollars in revenue even though my own list totaled 53 people (and some of those subscribers were relatives). After my launch, my database grew to a few thousand subscribers. People from other lists signed up for my newsletter. As a matter of fact, that was one of my bonus gifts for buying my book: a subscription to my newsletter.

#59: Research to Find the Perfect Partners for You

To benefit from partnering, you must be willing to do the work of finding potential partners and reaching out to them. The work is time-consuming but not difficult to do. When looking for potential partners, use your favorite search engine and search for keywords that match up your area of expertise or genre.

Create a chart to track your efforts in finding partners who have lists of followers. This can be done in either a Word processing program or Excel spreadsheet, whichever you are most comfortable using. Here are the columns I use:

1. Web site address of the partner
2. Keyword used to find this Web site on a search engine
3. Contact name, address, e-mail address
4. Do they have a newsletter? Do I subscribe?
5. Do they accept articles?
6. Do they do giveaways?
7. Comments and observations about site?
8. Date contacted

9. Date to follow up (use two columns as you may need to do it twice)
10. Response from site owner?
11. Commitment? When and how will he help?
12. Send personalized thank–you (fill in the date you did this)
13. Set up individual affiliate link (fill in the date you did this)

You might also leave a column for comments that can help you to follow up or to anticipate questions from the next potential partner you contact. In this way, you can refine your pitch to partners.

#60: Personalize Your Approach

Each and every e-mail, tweet, and social media post of yours should be friendly yet professional, reflecting your personal touch. If you send out impersonal communications you will keep your potential partners and customers at arm's length. Always look to make a personal connection. Reveal something about yourself that your partner can relate to without getting too personal and making people uncomfortable.

When approaching potential partners, never send an e-mail to "Dear potential partner," or use "Hello Everyone!" as your greeting. People want to be addressed by name (and they also want their name to be spelled properly). (I received an email from someone requesting my partnership and they called me "Cathy" in the salutation even though the email was addressed to peggy@destinies.com.) If you don't personally know the person you are reaching out to then take the time to go visit their Web site, research their name, find something that you have in common, and draw upon that when you send out a note. For example, when you go to their Web site and you see that they just recently released a book that is in alignment with your work, mention that in your e-mail.

If you are looking for support from a particular mentor, someone who has made a difference in your life, let this person know how much you appreciate him or her and offer a sincere compliment. However, do not put your mentors on a pedestal, as that only creates uncomfortable feelings. You'll have greater success if you reach out to potential partners as peers.

#61: Create a Bond and Instant Rapport

When you engage with folks, whether you are presenting from the stage, or via an e-mail or social media on the Internet, try to create instant report. Once you establish this, the relationship is golden. Gentle humor everyone can relate to is one way to break the ice. Another way is to ask people to answer a question or participate in your presentation in a fun, interesting way. For example, recently at a conference I had everyone in the room do the twist (to the song "Twist & Shout" by the Beatles) and called upon half a dozen people to come up on stage and show others how it is done. Everyone on stage felt like they were special and we created a unique bond. Following the conference, a number of people who were in the room said, "Peggy had everyone dancing in the aisles!"

Creating a bond with people helps to establish a relationship. People like to do business with people they like. Or, you may have heard the saying: people want to do business with people they like, respect, and trust. In Internet marketing, you need to bond right away with potential partners—and with your potential clients. Find common ground and bring it to their attention.

Get them "dancing" by asking them to stop what they are doing right now and take a moment to switch gears and connect to their passion and joy. For example, you might note that you share that person's enthusiasm for helping people to learn more about money management, reminding him or her of their passion. Make a connection and they may be eager to hear what else you have to say.

#62: Be Politely Persistent

As eager as you may be to partner with someone to get his or her assistance, at all times, be nice, polite, and patient with everyone. If you took away only one message from this book, please I ask you to remember the significance of being *politely* persistent. Don't become anxious and forget your manners. Trust that people will want to help you and take the time to be patient and friendly every time you ask a favor.

When you're reaching out to potential partners, especially people who have a substantial database or a large following, recognize that these are really busy people. If you sent an email or a message to someone and they haven't responded it isn't because they are ignoring you. They may not have seen your e-mail yet or the e-mail could have gone into a spam folder and they will never see it.

There are two other approaches you can politely try. You can see if you can find a telephone number on their Web site and call them. If you reach voice mail you could reference the e-mail and leave your e-mail address with the option for them to get back to you at their leisure. You could also let them know that you will send the e-mail again within the hour and ask them nicely to look for it. That may inspire them to pay attention to your e-mail and respond.

At what point do you finally give up trying to connect and partner with someone who could make a positive difference in your Internet marketing campaign? I would suggest you try several times and each time being extremely polite and kind. Very politely write again and say, "I know you are very busy but I thought I would write again and see if you have a moment now."

#63: Partners Want to Know WIIFM

Your partners want to know how they will benefit from partnering with you. In the early days of my business career, I was a sales person. My employer put me through sales school and one of the things we were taught is to imagine the initials WIIFM on the forehead of your prospect. If you were sitting across the desk from someone and there was something you wanted them to do (such as partner with you), you should imagine the initials WIIFM pasted on that person's forehead (signifying What's In It For Me?) and be fully prepared to answer that question.

When you are communicating to potential partners, get right to the point. Let your potential partners know how they will benefit from participating in your marketing campaign and let them know quickly. If you are offering a share of the revenue, and it is based on a percentage split, let them know what the potential earnings would be with different scenarios. The more they understand the benefit to them, the more successful you will be in getting them to agree to partner.

#64: Share the Revenue

Sharing the revenue with your partners creates a win/win scenario. You first need to determine what your costs are, the prices of your product, and the revenue split you are willing to live with. Some people are surprised when they learn of the big revenue share that is offered to partners. It isn't unusual to do a 50/50 split with a partner. You may ask, "Why would I give away 50 percent of the revenue?" I'm here to tell you why — without the partner you wouldn't have the business! It is as plain and simple as that. Remember earlier in the book we talked about the value of a customer. Your partners can connect you to customers you aren't able to access currently. And you may have an opportunity to sell your new customer something else down the road when he becomes a direct customer of your own and you don't have to share the revenue.

Some online marketers will split the revenue on every single sale their customer makes. In other words, if you gained a customer as a result of my e-mail list, and I earned a percentage of the revenue from the initial sale, each subsequent sale that came from that customer could also offer a revenue share. If you agree to this arrangement, you can keep track of sales to customers who originally came through someone else via shopping cart software. In other words, the shopping cart will actually keep track for you. The affiliate codes track the sales which makes it easier for everyone.

Also, partners will talk to each other. If one of your partners had a great experience partnering with you (for example, he generated significant revenues as a result), he may tell another list owner about you and that could lead to even more sales.

Be willing to share in the revenue and the partners will come.

#65: Your Potential Reach Constantly Increases

When you are looking for partners, and reach out to them, whether they have agreed to partner with you or not, ask them this question: "Do you know anyone else who would be an ideal partner for this opportunity?"

At the time of the writing of this book, there are over 122 million Web sites on the Internet. That number has never decreased and I suspect it will continue to increase in my lifetime. Sure, some sites may be dormant or be taken down, but new sites are coming online every single day. What does this mean to you? It means that your potential reach will never be exhausted. There isn't a person on this planet who can honestly stand up and claim that there aren't any more potential partners for their product and/or service.

And, while we are on the subject, there is no reason why you can't go back to existing partners and ask them to promote another product or the same product again. I have one partner who has promoted my product with five separate mailings and each and every time has generated healthy sales and earned some wonderful affiliate commissions.

#66: Finding Partners Is an Ongoing Process As Is Learning How to Do Successful Marketing Campaigns

Part of being a successful Internet marketer is having the vision and part is taking action. Many people get ideas but they don't do anything about them, or they begin to take action but soon lose interest. Partnering is an ongoing process so you should always envision getting new partners. Look for them everywhere. Sign up for newsletters and check out Web sites in your area of expertise.

When I see there is an affiliate opportunity coming up as a result of someone sending me an e-mail and it looks compelling (well done and organized), I will sign up to be an affiliate even if I end up not promoting it, that is, participating in the launch by sending out an e-mail to my list. I'll keep e-mails regarding that launch in a folder and watch how the launch is being built before making my decision. After all, I only want to promote products and services to my followers if I truly believe in their value.

Many successful affiliate campaigns have contests for the affiliate who generates the greatest number of leads, or the most revenue. During the process, the affiliate manager will post the winners of the contest, thus giving you insight into who has the most effective lists. These are list owners you will probably want to partner with for your upcoming launch. This list of effective partners could be gold for you.

CHAPTER 8

OTHER WAYS TO REACH YOUR MARKET

There are numerous ways to reach your market, build your visibility, and become recognized as an expert and you can do this as quickly as you wish. At the end of the day, it really is up to you whether you are going to execute the marketing ideas that have been presented to you in this book. But, I will tell you this: If you do follow through you'll be amazed and excited at the results.

What's more, the principles I'm offering you can be applied to many situations. The opportunities to reach prospects online are enormous and continue to expand. Open your mind to the possibilities!

#67: Be Everywhere

I remember once receiving an e-mail from someone asking me, "Who is doing your Internet marketing?" I sent back a response and asked why they were inquiring (I wasn't sure if they were impressed by my marketing or if they were about to complain!). As it turned out, they were completely impressed because they were seeing my name and my book everywhere!

When I'm launching a product, I will do an Internet marketing campaign that involves getting the word out through e-mail blasts, having it talked about on blogs and reviewed on Web sites and social media sites, and having my articles and book excerpts circulating around. In addition, I'll also use other methods to expand my reach such as teleseminars, radio shows, speaking engagements, magazine and newspaper interviews, and television appearances.

If someone hears about your product once, they may buy it. If they hear about it twice, they are likely to have the impression that your product is very important and successful, and they will make a point of checking it out. If they hear about it multiple times, it definitely catches their attention. Haven't you felt excited when someone mentioned to you an event, film, product, or idea you have already heard about? You start to think you and the other person are "on to" something big. Market everywhere online and you will not only have your message heard once but more than once by a potential customer, increasing the "buzz" about what you are selling.

#68: Blogging Helps You Build Your Credibility and Sell Products

Many marketers have bought into the idea that blogging is a valuable part of the overall inbound marketing strategy. Blogging builds your credibility and reputation as a leader and original thinker. It also helps you become a powerful magnet for new visitors and generates leads for your business.

There are many benefits to blogging:

- Builds your brand
- Establishes your credibility and expertise
- Adds new content to your site, which improves search engine rankings (if the blog is located on, or teased on, your site).

- Encourages prospects to get to know your content, helping them become more connected to you and more likely to invest in your products
- May create an interactive community
- May attract media interest in you and your business
- Establishes the beginning of reciprocity: You are giving away valuable information for free and eventually people will feel comfortable giving back to you through supporting your offerings

Promote your blog through an RSS feed ("really simple syndication"), which lets fans of your site know immediately when you have posted a new blog piece. You can also post notification of a new blog piece on social media sites and inform your newsletter subscribers.

Remember, too, that you can do a video blog as well as a text blog, and you can invite comments to get a dialogue going and create a sense of community.

#69: Repurpose Your Blog Content

There are many opportunities to communicate and share your messages through multiple platforms by repurposing your blog content. For example, every month, I generate eight new blogs pieces. Each one could be used as a stand-alone article and be posted on multiple Web sites that host expert articles. I've also taken excerpts from my books and used them as blog pieces, and allowed other bloggers to share my information by posting these pieces on their own sites. In addition, my blog pieces have often served as articles used on popular Web sites and in other people's newsletters.

You can also take some of your content from your audio interviews, have them transcribed, and create blog pieces from them. You could pull together multiple blog entries into one eBook or eReport and sell it from your Web site. Although you may feel your blog piece is familiar because you have used it in one, two, or three places, it will feel fresh and new to most people, so repurpose it again and again.

#70: Use Media to Drive Traffic to Your Site and Sell Products

One of the best experts on using media to drive traffic to his Web site (and make sales!) is Alex Carroll. Alex is brilliant when it comes to radio publicity and he shares with other experts on the methods he has used to get results from being interviewed on the radio. It is wonderful to be interviewed and be featured on radio, but if it doesn't achieve results, is it really worth your time? Maybe, or maybe not. But, if you are going to be getting exposure on media, why not use it to drive traffic to your site and sell a product or service, or give something away to your visitors so that you can capture their e-mail addresses?

When you are on the air, let people know the address of your Web site and give them a reason for going there. Make sure your domain name is easy to remember and if it isn't, get an easy-to-remember domain name and set it up to redirect people to your Web site. Most people listening to radio are in their car and they may not have access to a pen, hence the reason to have a memorable URL (Web site address). You could say "go to my Web site right now and get the top 5 tips for...." And clearly communicate your Web site's address by both saying it and spelling it out.

#71: Be a Guest on Other People's Teleseminars

There are many teleseminar series being offered on a regular basis and they can provide terrific exposure for you. When you see one that resonates with you and fits your area of expertise, contact the organizer and offer to be featured in their teleseminar series. The host may ask you to promote the teleseminar in an e-mail to your database.

Typically the way these teleseminars work is that one person (or a couple of people) put them together and bring together like-minded individuals who are experts in their field who agree to be interviewed and promote the event. When the teleseminar series features multiple speakers (these series are called "summits"), the overall exposure is going to be huge and beneficial for all involved. Confidently reach out to the organizers and let them know why you would be a beneficial addition to their offering.

#72: Create Your Own Teleseminar Series

A number of my clients have offered their own teleseminar series. This type of offering is also called a "summit." If you are just starting out, and have a passion for a particular field, you might bring together several experts and like-minded individuals and offer your own series.

The revenue from teleseminar series or summits is generated from the sale of the recorded interviews and from special offerings that each featured speaker makes available at the conclusion of the call (which consists of the host interviewing the expert and fielding calls from listeners). Provided that the event is put together professionally, promoted heavily, and delivered respectfully, and provided that it gives great value, the revenues usually come in droves.

#73: Have Your Articles Included in Others' Newsletters

Write articles, repurpose blog pieces, take excerpts from your book, and offer them as content for newsletters that have a big reach.

Do your research and find the newsletters that are popular and have a big subscriber base. For instance, you might do a search for "Top Web sites" and the keyword for your subject area.

How do you know how large a particular site's subscriber base is? You can ask the creator of the newsletter. Sometimes newsletters will list the number of subscribers right in the beginning of the newsletter. If someone is producing a newsletter on a regular basis, they have a challenge to create new, engaging, informative and relevant information and you can help. You can help them by providing some great content that their subscribers may love. This approach is very effective and can give you terrific exposure to potential customers.

At the conclusion of your articles, create a "call to action." Ask people to go to your Web site and sign up for your subscriber list so they can receive a free gift, or write a couple lines of marketing copy that drives traffic back to your site. Articles in others' newsletters may help you build your e-mail list, as they will drive traffic to your Web site. They can also help you sell your products and/or services as long as your site clearly directs visitors to take that action.

#74: Have Articles on Popular Web Sites

At a recent event, Arianna Huffington of the Huffington Post offered everyone in the audience an opportunity to submit an article and potentially have a blog on this very popular site. I was a speaker at the same event and decided to take her up on the offer. I submitted an article following Arianna's advice and within one week I had a regular blog on Huffington Post!

Web site owners require fresh, valuable content for their sites. When you provide that, they benefit, so be confident and approach popular Web sites. Ask them if they will take your articles or feature your blog.

How do you know if the Web site is popular or not? Go to a site that ranks Web sites such as www.alexa.com and enter the domain name. You'll be shown the actual statistics of visitors and unique visitors to the site.

#75: Go to Industry Events, Introduce Yourself to People, and Interact with Them

Even though we have this wonderful vehicle called the Internet that allows us to reach out and instantly connect with people anywhere on the globe, it's still essential that you attend live events in your genre. This allows you to be seen, connect, and create new relationships.

Most events require participants to wear a badge, making it easy to start a conversation with a stranger. You will find plenty of time for networking at these live events and meet people who can help you with ideas, advice, and support. You may connect with a partner that becomes one of your biggest affiliates. I would also suggest that even if you are not speaking at the event, connect with the speakers as well. Say hello, introduce yourself, and thank them for coming to speak. Ask a question or simply make the connection with a compliment. When I attended my very first book marketing event several years ago, I made an extra effort to personally introduce myself to all of the speakers and have my photo taken with them. I can confidently say that today most of them are my close friends and these relationships have contributed significantly to my success.

CHAPTER 9

CUSTOMER LOYALTY

As much as the Internet provides an enormous opportunity to reach millions and millions of people, it also offers a challenge: How can you stand out from the rest? The answer is that you have to create and offer superior products and services that people need (or very strongly desire), you have to make it easy for people to buy from you, you must offer great prices, and you must deliver top-notch customer service.

Some people make money selling inferior products, but they don't stay in business very long unless they work exceptionally hard to constantly find new customers. Customers today are very savvy. They know when they have gotten a deal and they know when they have gotten ripped off.

By cultivating a loyal customer base, you protect the future of your business.

#76: Offer a Money Back Guarantee—No Questions Asked

When I started out marketing on the Internet, one of my mentors told me, "You will increase your business by 50 percent or more if you offer a 100 percent unconditional money-back guarantee." He was right! Having this type of guarantee demonstrates that you stand behind what you are selling. It shows that you have complete confidence and trust in your product or service. More importantly it allows your customers and potential customers to feel a greater sense of confidence. Knowing that the risk of being taken advantage of or sold an inferior product is almost nonexistent, they will be much more likely to buy.

Be open to the idea that you may not necessarily believe they deserve to get their money back. Some people just can't be satisfied, no matter what. However, one person speaking negatively about you and/or your business can have a profound effect. On the other hand, if you graciously refund his money, that person may tell others,

"The service wasn't for me but I'll say this, they stand by their word to give you your money back if you aren't fully satisfied." People are impressed by integrity. Also, a money-back guarantee can generate so many extra sales.

Will people ask for their money back? Possibly. It has happened to me on very rare occasions. And when they ask, I respond with warmth and honor the guarantee as promised.

#77: Respond Quickly to Payment Problems

The key to a successful relationship is to be attentive to your customers and respond in a timely manner to their inquiries, *especially* if they involve payment problems. It shows that you believe that they are important. On those rare occasions when people have asked me for their money back, I provide an immediate credit (if they paid by credit card), transfer the funds back (if they paid by Paypal), or send them a check. As much as this seems to be such a simple thing to do, you will be amazed how few people actually do it, much less in timely fashion.

The only challenge with this is that the credit card companies seem to take their own sweet time processing credits and even though you may have applied the credit upon request, for some strange reason, it can take a couple of weeks before their credit shows up at the other end (although you may see the credit at your end right away). As a courtesy, you may want to let your client know that it may take a couple of extra weeks for the credit card company to show the credit. This way, you avoid any surprises and won't leave your customer further dissatisfied.

#78: No Customer Should Go Away Unhappy

Bill and Steve Harrison, who run a successful business called Bradley Communications, offer a policy of "no customer goes away unhappy." If a customer requests his money back, not only do they refund the money in a timely manner, they learn from the experience to see what they can do better in the future to avoid an unhappy customer. They also offer that customer some type of bonus gift, such as entry to a future event for no charge, a free ad in their RTIR magazine, or something else of value.

When I first learned of this, I thought they were extremely generous, but they said that they know the value of their reputation and they want to be sure every customer is happy, whether he has asked for and been given a refund or not. I'm constantly impressed with the high level of service that Steve and Bill offer their customers and they have taught me some of the most valuable business lessons I've learned in my career.

So although you may never meet your customers, make sure you always leave them with a positive impression of you and your business.

#79: Manage Your Customers' Expectations

When you are first starting out in your new venture it may feel strange and unwise to turn down business. Have you ever thought or heard yourself say, *"She already seems difficult to work with, but I really need the money."* or, *"John referred him to me so I had better just stick with it."* or, *"I am new at this. Who am I to turn down business?"*

Let's take the emotion out of this equation for a minute. In most cases, the responsibility for your clients' success is theirs. Whether you are coaching, collaborating, or marketing for them, they have to contribute to the process. If you promise, or they imply, otherwise, you are walking into quicksand. That is not to say you shouldn't be seen as a part of the solution, but you are not to blame if they don't do the required work and thus do not achieve positive results.

"If it is to be it is up to me."—William H. Johnsen

There it is: ten words, only two letters each. I love this quote because it so simply reaffirms my point.

Be very clear with your clients: "Here's my role and here's your role." As a coach and mentor to my clients, I guide them in developing the skills that they are struggling to develop. Taking action is up to them.

Always remember that your job is not to fix or rescue someone or his business but to provide helpful services and products.

#80: Hire Others to Help You

Certain aspects of your business might be better handled by an outside source. As we mentioned earlier in the book, if you are not familiar with how to write great marketing copy, hire a copywriter; if you do not have the skills or knowledge to create a great web page, hire a web designer.

If you are not available or able to offer superior customer service, and you may not be great at dealing with customers, find someone who is and hire that person to take care of this role for you. You could have this person on an as-needed-basis and pay them by the hour or by the project. My husband often tells me that he wouldn't be the person to handle customer service issues. He knows that and honors it. He does help me in my business by taking care of some of the product shipments and other things, but he often says, *"Don't ever put me in charge of customer service."*

#81: Ask Your Customers How You May Serve Them Better

People feel valued and appreciated when asked for their opinion or feedback on how they may serve you better. Even a satisfied customer may be able to offer you valuable constructive criticism that can help you in the future, but he is likely not to speak up unless you actually ask, "Is there any way I might serve you better in the future".

Ask your customers what they need and how you may serve them more effectively. You might create a survey and offer multiple choices for answers. For example, I surveyed my own database once and asked the clients if they preferred to have teleseminars during the evening, on a weekday, or on the weekend. I assumed clients preferred having teleseminars during the week, but was surprised to find out their preference was for weekend teleseminars.

Note: If you are offering teleseminars and you have people from all over the world signing up, you may want to be respectful of time zones overseas. Of course, I always record my teleseminars so that customers can listen to them at their leisure even if they can't participate in "real time."

Most people don't like criticism and there may be times when a customer offers you some suggestions and in an appropriate fashion, for example, they might seem nitpicky or aggressive. Look past the emotion of the customer and determine whether theirs is a valid idea. Whenever you receive a suggestion, thank your customer and promise to consider it even if you are tempted to immediately dismiss it. Perhaps their suggestion won't seem workable at first but as you think about it more, you will find in it the gem of a great idea for improving your products and services. Remain open-minded, and be grateful for all feedback.

#82: Stay Open to Ways to Improve Products and Delivery

There is one constant in this life and that is change. Always be open to new ideas, whether it is the product itself or the method that you use to market it. Even simple little changes will open up doors so that you can re-launch a product or offer it at a special price.

I deliver a lot of teleseminars but webinars are becoming more and more popular. If it serves my audience better to deliver one of my programs in a webinar format, I'll switch to that format in order to improve the delivery. As you look at your own products and services, think about the many different delivery and packaging options you might offer. Then, try to solicit feedback from your customers. If they enjoy what you have to offer, they are likely to have some very clever suggestions for how you can provide them with even more value.

#83: Watch the Market and Your Competition

Thanks to the Internet, it is easier than ever to learn what others in your industry are doing and to learn from their successes, challenges, and failures. It is also easy to learn what is new in technology. A problem that you have been wrestling with for some time may be easily fixed by a new application or software program that others in your field have already discovered. Or, they may have happened across a new business model that you might use effectively for your own benefit. For example, if they are offering an affiliate program with a revenue split, how are they setting up payments and what splits are they offering to various affiliates—and what is the reasoning behind this particular model?

Once you have discovered who the big players are in your industry, the easiest and simplest way to watch them is to go to their site and sign up to be on their mailing list. Watch and learn from them. See how they are serving their clients; check out the products and/or services they are bringing to the market and the way they are promoting them. You can learn a lot by simply observing others. Model success but stay on top of how people are achieving success.

CHAPTER 10

HOW SOCIAL MEDIA CAN ADD TO YOUR BOTTOM LINE

Social media has grown in popularity to unsurpassed numbers, similar to the rapid growth of the World Wide Web in the 1990s. In the early days of social media sites, I wondered if they were time wasters and perhaps a fad. After all, some of them began as fun sites for college students to exchange music and gossip. However, soon I realized that not only was social media here to stay but that it had enormous potential for helping people to market on the Internet. Social media is now recognized as one of the most highly accessible and widely used ways to turn communication into interactive dialogue with clients, potential customers, leaders in your field, and colleagues. If you are not using social media now, you definitely need to be. Learning how to use it effectively for Internet marketing and building your brand and your business should be top priority.

I am not suggesting you jump on the social media "technology bandwagon" simply because it is trendy. You may find that certain social media sites are more effective for your purposes than others are. When assessing the various sites, a good question to ask yourself is the following, "Will this medium help me build my brand, expand my business, serve my clients more effectively or do something that enhances my customer service offering?" If the answer is "yes," invest the time to learn how to use it effectively and start engaging.

#84: Be Consistent

When you are ready to use social media, you need to make a commitment to use it on a regular basis. If you create a presence on them and then disappear, you might confuse customers and even hurt your business. Imagine opening a store, getting people interested in what you have, and then closing the door without notice or any explanation. Prospects may think your business folded, or they may not think about you at all. If your time is tight and you need a break from regular posting, you have two options. First, you can post a notification to your followers that you are taking a short break, but if you do so, let them know when you will be back and return to posting on that day. This is a good strategy if, say, you will be taking a vacation, are working on a deadline, or have to devote more attention to your personal life (for example, if a family member becomes ill). Another way to take a break is to continue to post but keep it simple. Post quotations or links to interesting articles that you come across in the course of your day, post short excerpts from blogs, articles, or books you have written, or post a link to something already on your Web site such as an archived newsletter. You can repost others' posts (to do this, follow people in your field who post links of interest) to your own followers, which takes very little time. Just be sure to check in for a few minutes on any social media site where followers can publicly respond to your posts. You don't want someone posting spam or an inappropriate or hostile comment, and besides, if someone asks a question you may want to give a quick response. Never completely ignore your social media sites unless you have specifically told your followers you need to do so for a short period of time.

You establish customer loyalty by being present, connected, and engaged on the social media sites. You also build, maintain, and even grow your brand on social media sites. Keep your messaging consistent on all sites and remember that everything you post online is a representation of you and your business. Cross post so that those who consistently use one site and not another do not miss any of your posts. There are software programs that allow your posts from one site to appear on another, and you can set up your blog or Web site to feature your latest posts, too. Don't neglect your followers on one site simply because you're more comfortable using another. Learn about them all so that you can contact and interact with prospects and clients on all of them.

Be forewarned than *anything* you post on a social media site might be accessed by someone you don't know. Although privacy settings help you control access, they change all the time, so proceed with caution. A friend of mine posted an opinion on a local news article on her friend's

Facebook wall. She stated that she felt that the local government shouldn't have bailed out a company that had a fundamental flaw in their business model. The next thing she knew, a representative of that company launched a personal attack against her on the wall, using harsh language. She posted, "I am sorry you feel that way but I disagree." In taking her opinion personally, this businessman missed an opportunity to build goodwill and enhance his company's reputation and, in fact, left a terrible impression for many to read. Now, this same friend of mine also posted in the comments section on a large blog that she was hesitant to use a particular product because she was unsure of how safe it was. A representative of the company, who clearly had a search engine alert set up for her brand's name, posted a pleasant response informing my friend of the safety testing that her company does and offering her a free sample of the product. My friend was not just impressed, but she went on to promote that product to her own followers. Now that's how to use social media to market effectively and build your brand!

Note that if you look at privacy settings on the sites, you'll see that you can limit who sees your photos, profile, or posts. Use these settings judiciously. On Facebook, you can set up lists of followers so that if you choose to post something for family and close friends, they will see your post, and you can block your clients from seeing it. This is especially helpful if you have different groups of followers and more than one brand you represent because limiting the number of posts that a particular group might not be interested in prevents "information overload" that can lead to people "hiding" your posts or choosing to stop following you. If you are hosting a local event, you might choose to announce it to all your followers, but post only to those who are local when you want to give reminders.

#85: The Biggest Part to Social Media is Engaging with Others

Simply posting information or sharing tips is not making the best use of your social media experience. You need to engage with others. Ask people for their opinions and to share their comments, and respond when people do comment. Engage with others when you see something you like in their social media accounts. In this way, you will encourage people to follow you *and* you may receive valuable feedback that helps you adjust your message, gives you an idea for a blog or a new product, or simply helps you feel inspired.

I have found that people are pleasantly surprised when I respond to their messages on social media sites. From time to time, someone will say, *"I can't believe it is really you responding!"* Remember that saying, "people don't care how much you know until they know how much you care." This statement couldn't be more appropriate for using social media. Engaging with others shows you care. Once you do that, people will be far more interested in what you know and what you have to offer.

#86: Find Influencers and Engage with Them

If you are new to social media or if your following isn't substantial, you can use this technique to rapidly grow your number of followers and increase your connections on the social media sites. Determine who are the influencers on the social media sites – they have the most people following them. Find the people in your field who are the most influential and engage with them. You can respond to their posts and forward their messages and share with others (credit them so that they know you are helping promote their own brand). It may take a short period of time, or it may take a while, but sooner or later if the influencer is someone who is engaging with others on the social media sites, they will connect with you. Ask someone to befriend you or connect with you, but do so in a personal way rather than sending an unsolicited request with no note. (And yes, your colleague from ten years ago may not recognize your name so be sure to remind her of who you are before asking her to link to you much less recommend you.)

Once again, learn from successful models. Which influencers' posts seem to generate the greatest number of responses? What type of material are they sharing with others? What seems to excite their followers and get people engaged and talking? Who have they connected to online, and should you be connecting with those "movers and shakers" as well?

#87: Stay on Your Social Toes

Social media sites are always changing to serve their users more effectively. This means that you need to keep up with the changes so that you have a more beneficial social media experience. Staying on your social media toes means staying on top of trends and new developments so that you can take advantage of them to grow your business. There may be new features on social media sites that may not be of interest to you at first but as you learn more about them, observing how others are using them, you can learn how to work with these new features in a beneficial way and learn which ones are simply time wasters.

Stay in touch with people in your industry and ask them what they think of a new social media feature. Offer your experiences. You might find that one social media site is more effective for building a certain type of following than another is. You might also realize that what seems like a purely social feature has business applications. Share information and experiences with others who are using social media for business and you will save yourself a lot of time and wasted effort.

#88: Make It Easy for People to Connect with You

You can offer your social media buttons and connections on all of the places you have a web presence and suggest people connect with you. On your Web site, you can place buttons and links to the popular social media sites where you are active. As you learned earlier in the book, tell people what you want them to do: "connect with me" "follow me" "join" "like my page" (use whatever is the proper verbiage for the different sites and stay on top of it because it changes). Have those social media buttons on your blog site, too. If you have a newsletter, make a recommendation to your subscribers to connect with you on social media. Send out e-mails to your customer database (people who have purchased from you previously) asking them to connect with you.

Create auto responders when people buy from you and recommend they connect with you (be sure to include the links to your sites and social media sites). Have customized pages created on the social media sites so that people can see what other social media sites you're on. As part of your signature on your e-mails, include links to your Web site or blog and links for your pages on social media with a recommendation to "follow me." Include links on your business card too. Everywhere you are, let people know the many ways they can connect with you.

#89: Advertise on Social Media

In addition to sharing information, resources, ideas, tips, and strategies on the social media sites, these sites also offer you the opportunity to promote your products and services via ads.

When I was preparing for one of my book launches, which was a free event in Ottawa, Ontario, I was able to run ads on the social media sites that targeted people within a geographical area. You can also run ads targeting people with certain keywords in their profile, or who fit into a particular demographic. Become familiar with creating and using targeted ads on social media as these sites have gained and will continue to gain in popularity. They offer you the opportunity to reach hundreds of millions of people, or thousands of people who are the perfect target market for you. Of course, as you know from the copywriting chapter in this book, you must use effective copywriting techniques to persuade people to take action and learn more about your product, event, or service. Notice which ads you respond to and why.

#90: Keep Your Videos Short and Sweet

Online video sharing sites have exploded in popularity. The number of videos that are uploaded every minute is staggering. Millions and millions of people are watching them.

One key to creating great viral videos is to keep them short. People's attention spans are very limited. Perhaps you've had the experience of someone sending you an intriguing video but as soon as you clicked on it and realized it was many minutes long, you turned it off because you didn't want to devote that much time to watching it. On the other hand, if someone has sent you a short video, you probably *did* check it out.

How long is too long? Again, your best bet is to check successful models. Informational videos will run longer than videos that serve as greetings. Funny videos are often very short—after a couple of minutes, you have probably seen enough cute animal tricks. The more that is going on in a video, the easier it is to watch it. Footage of a person talking into a web cam for many minutes is not as interesting as a video of that same person talking, interspersed with graphics, Power Point-type slides, and the like.

#91: Give Your Video Watchers an Action to Take

When making a video to build your brand and establish your credibility, tell your viewer what action you want him or her to take. Let's say you want a "welcome" video of yourself on the home page of your Web site. Introduce yourself and talk about your business, but then encourage people to check out the site, sign up for your newsletter, buy your book, and so on.

Or, let's say you want to create an engaging, informational video, or a funny one that goes viral simply because it is so enjoyable to watch. Make sure that at the end you ask the viewer to take action. You might have a "title card" that tells people to visit your Web site and provides the URL (address). You might get across your information with animated text. Whether you want people to buy your book, or go to your Web site, or get the free download, or tell ten friends, make your directions clear.

#92: Make Your Videos Engaging

You do not have to be Steven Spielberg to make an engaging or even entertaining video that gets across your message to potential customers. There are a number of elements you can incorporate to ensure that your promotional video grabs your viewer's attention and holds it. You don't need to use all of them—even using just one will make your video more engaging.

1. **Unbelievable:** Your message contains something that is shocking (in a good or bad way) or unexpected.
2. **Curious:** Your video interests people and gets them thinking, talking, and perhaps even wanting more (having their curiosity stimulated is a big motivator for people so don't underestimate it).
3. **Brilliantly created:** Your message is clever and intelligently presented (it may not be "new" information but you've found a way to share something with others in a unique way).
4. **Funny and Entertaining:** Your video makes people smile or laugh.
5. **Exciting Due to its Mind-blowing Offer:** You present an offer so attractive that it ex-

cites people and causes them to share it with others.

6. **Unorthodox:** Your message is different from what others are saying or thinking, and may even be controversial.

7. **Unusual:** The video is unusual, strange, interesting, and creative, and it fascinates people.

8. **Deeply needed:** The video offers something people are hungry for. It holds a promise for solving a very common problem easily, quickly, and better than anyone else can

9. **Adds value:** Your video serves as a resource that helps people's lives and it clearly demonstrates value.

10. **Brief:** Again, people have short attention spans. Do not make your video any longer than it needs to be to convey your message.

In video, you may wish to make claims about your products or services. As with any online marketing, it is imperative that you follow the FTC guidelines and communicate ethically, legally, and honestly.

#93: Business Social Media Sites

There are now social media sites that are targeted to professionals. These sites provide a way to build a powerful social network and connect with industry professionals, especially business to business. People use business social media sites to stay in contact and communicate with co-workers and industry peers, get business advice, and even find new jobs. These sites can be a great place to make your relevant business contacts aware of your brand. However, just as with the other social media sites, there are things you need to do and not do. Don't promote yourself too aggressively; don't join or participate in groups unless you want to be associated with them; do not leave your profile blank; make sure you optimize your profile for search engine optimization; be sure to promote your business social media sites on your Web site; do not ignore connection invitations; and be sure to post status updates regularly. And remember to engage with others!

#94: How to Create a Positive Flash Mob

Have you heard the stories of teenagers texting their friends to announce a party at someone's house, only to find out that one text was sent to another teen and to another and the next thing you know hundreds of unexpected guests arrive at the teenager's home? Too many of these stories are in the media, and the reason is because these unexpected parties get out of control. Complete strangers show up, alcohol may be involved, and fights emerge. This is an example of a negative flash mob. However, as an online marketer, you can take advantage of social media tools to create a *positive* flash mob.

There is great power in person–to-person communication that leads to a chain of communication. You can use this to your advantage. Let's say you are offering a sale for a limited time or hosting a special event. You could text someone and ask them to text three of their friends to pass along the message. Actually request that a chain reaction occur to see if you can use this medium of texting to reach massive amounts of people. You never know—you could actually create a positive flash mob that shows up at your event or your site.

CHAPTER 11

WAIT 5 MINUTES— THINGS WILL CHANGE

I love to study the Internet and observe how things are changing and evolving. I am watching it all of the time and examining what has worked for marketers and how the average person can duplicate the successful models. It has become an addiction for me to study success, and when I became involved with marketing online, it fed my interest in technology.

I've had the pleasure of helping thousands of people be successful on the Internet, as well as creating my own success by marketing on the Internet. I've taken several of my own books to the top of the best-seller lists, including earning the notable *New York Times Best Selling Author* title. I've also taken several of my client's books to the top of the best-seller lists (which also included making their books New York Times Best-Sellers). For years, I have always wanted to share with people what's happening online and what's hot. At the end of the day, the question for me has always been, "What does it do to the bottom line?" I have to consider whether it helps me serve my customers, make new offerings, or expand my business and build my brand.

There are things about Internet marketing that will change but the fundamentals of marketing will always stay the same. Your job as an Internet marketer is to keep applying the principles of success even as the terrain of the Internet transforms.

Find people who can offer you simple principles for using these new technologies and explain how to apply them. Keep in mind that there are three levels of learning. The first level is to seek to find the information, the next is to understand it, and the third level is to implement it. You can't go from the first level to the third level without understanding the information.

Be patient with yourself as you learn new technologies. You will be pleasantly surprised to find lots of resources available online to help you understand technological advances. You don't need to be the trendsetter, although you could be, but watch how others use new technology so that you might replicate their success.

#95: Changes in Internet Marketing Are Exciting, Yet Challenging

Many people resist change and respond to it negatively out of fear, but the changes in Internet marketing are all to be welcomed. Internet changes and the rapid growth in the possibilities for Internet marketing are exciting because it keeps us on our toes and gets our creative juices flowing. I find that I'm never bored working in my industry. I also find that working with my clients and creating offers and marketing online doesn't get boring. For the most part, marketing on the Internet is easy. If it wasn't, people probably wouldn't be doing it. Gone are the days of "business as usual."

Sometimes I tell people that my middle name is "flexible." I'll say, *"You can call me Peggy 'Flexible' McColl."* I have to be flexible in the way I serve, how I market, and how I conduct

145

my business overall. If I weren't flexible, I be-lieve I'd be left behind... and being left behind is not something that I have any inclination to ex-perience!

I'm grateful that I am amenable to change be-cause there is no avoiding it. If you are resistant to change and focused on the challenges of keep-ing up with the ever-changing Internet rather than the opportunities, you may want to adopt a perspective of curiosity tempered by caution. Allow yourself to increase your own sense of fascination and approach the new changes with a fun and playful spirit. Don't be afraid to try out new social media sites or technologies, but don't feel pressured to master them immediately either. Keep it fun. It is easier to learn when you're finding the process enjoyable.

You could designate a specific amount of time each week to learning new methods of marketing on the Internet. Decide that it will be your play-ful hour (or hours) of investigative time and learn what you can about the new changes and updates to the way people are connecting and serving their clients online. If you do happen to have an assistant, you may want to get your as-sistant to do this for you. Have him or her do the research and provide you with a summary report. That could save you a lot of time.

#96: Keep Things Simple with Easy-to-use Technology

If you find technology difficult to use, you can expect that your customers will, too. One of my clients was told she should begin a blog on a new, trendy blog hosting site. Although she found it easy to design a beautiful looking blog, she had difficulty getting the commenting software to work. She had a few of her friends try leaving comments, following the software prompts, but it was soon clear that the complex software would serve as a barrier to interaction with her clients. She closed down that particular blog and moved it over to a more user-friendly Web site. After experimenting with that one a bit, she realized it was far easier to use and felt comfortable announcing her new blog to her followers. "Trendy" just wasn't as important to her followers and her as how easy it was to use.

I've observed that some people tend to want to make tasks and projects more difficult than they have to be. For example, when offering a product online, you need to have a method for payment authorization. If the shopping cart you are using or the payment method isn't easy to use, people will leave. They simply don't want to work that hard to figure out how to operate the shopping cart function and check out. Their impatience could be costing you business.

When I searched for payment methods for my own Web site, I looked for shopping carts that had rave reviews from users. Functionality was important but one of my own criteria for making a buying decision was to find a shopping cart that other users weren't just satisfied with but actually thrilled with. If they weren't thrilled with the product, how could I expect to be?

I also have found that I prefer to have my Web site in a format that allows me to easily upload changes and not have to bother my web master for each and every little tweak. You've read in this book about the importance of changing and updating your site on a regular basis to keep things fresh. If you can do these changes yourself, that is even better because you won't have to depend on your web designer being available or following your directions to the "T." One of my clients found that when he let his web designer create new links and upload pages, the designer kept using the terminology "press here" instead of "click here." Because my client is a writer, he was particular about using "click here" as the term. Uploading his own pages made it easier for him to avoid having to ask his web master to attend to what might seem to many to be minor details but which were important to my client given that people judge him by his writing and editing. Colin Miller, my web master, tends to be very accessible, but I don't want to bother him all of the time for little things, so he has set up my Web sites so that I can make changes as I wish.

#97: Find Mentors and Coaches

We are constantly evolving beings. Just like our businesses, we are either getting better or getting worse. We are the ones who decide which direction we're going in—the direction of growth or the opposite direction. If you think that staying stagnant is safe, you need to think again. It is one of the worse things you can do. You need to develop the attitude of finding ways to improve in your business and as a professional, if you do, your results will change in a positive way.

I have a mentor to help me in my business. He is a very successful businessman. I chose someone who has achieved tremendous success and done so with total integrity. Integrity is one of my highest values and must be a part of my life and business, so I chose to find a mentor who was like-minded and highly successful. It makes sense to work with a mentor who is achieving better results than you are. They have already learned the lessons of success, and they can share them with you, which will save you both time and money.

I also have a speaking coach. He helps me with my presentation techniques. He works with me on customizing my presentation materials and delivery. I have found that working with him has improved my skills in this area, helped me feel more relaxed about speaking, and even caused me to enjoy it so much more. More importantly, my audience gets more out of my presentations and that is what it is all about.

As an Internet marketer, you need to create and promote products, services, and your brand effectively. Whatever your strengths are, you will have some weaknesses. We all do. Consider working with a mentor or coach to help you where you have challenges and you will soon find that some of your weaknesses have actually become strengths. And remember, hiring a coach does not mean you are not skilled in a particular area. It simply means that whatever your skill level, you are looking to improve.

#98: Don't Ignore What's "Hot"

Technology will always change. Some people, called "first adapters" or "early adapters," are quick to pick up on the hottest trends in technology while others are a little slower to invest time and money in what's new and "hot." Others are still mourning the loss of typewriters!

I have seen many technology changes over the years, and believe me, some of the "hot" new "must have" items soon became cold, but many took off in a huge way. When I graduated from high school, I started working on a mini computer. My career lead me to work for a mini computer manufacturer which gave me the perfect exposure to learn this technology. Word processing equipment evolved after the mini-computer rage. Following that, micro computers emerged. Laptop computers followed; then tele-communications; then data communications; and then the Internet! Prior to working in my own business, my career was in these leading technologies. By keeping up with technology and what's "hot," I was able to quickly grow in my career and earn top dollar.

Staying in touch with technology makes you more valuable to your clients. You don't have to be at the cutting edge at all times, but you do have to keep up and try to be an "early adapter," learning about new technologies and their applications soon after they come out.

What does staying on top of technology innovations mean to your bottom line? Increasing revenues. Growing a business is imperative. If your business isn't growing it is fading away, so stay up to date with the latest technology.

You can stay up to date on technology by showing up at events in your industry, you can also stay on top of technology by attending the leading technology events. There are numerous events offered and you can either attend "virtually" (online) or in person. Either way, make it a part of your business development to attend and learn and connect at popular industry events.

Even if you are not that familiar with all of the technology, I guarantee you, when you start to attend industry and technology events and become a sponge for learning about the latest trends, it won't be long before you have a grasp on it.

#99: Be a Leader in Your Field

People love to work with leaders. Leaders demonstrate confidence, which is an attractive and attracting emotion. Not everyone has confidence, so when they see someone who embodies it, they want to connect with that person. John Assaraf, a very successful businessman, has become a great friend of mine. I admire that he has built many businesses and achieved tremendous success. John is a leader in his field because he stays focused on the fundamentals of a successful business, he provides excellent customer service, and he is always on top of the latest technologies. John doesn't sit back and ride on his success. He has grabbed the success bull by the horns and taken charge. He demonstrates and inspires confidence.

If you are just starting out in business, create a presence and the persona of a leader. Let others know through your messaging that you are a leader and demonstrate it. If you are confident in your information, guidance, and approach, take a stand and become a leader in your field. Others will benefit from your expertise and you will build your business due to your reputation.

Another way to establish yourself as a leader in your field, is to get out of the virtual world and into the real world and speak, present, or be a panelist at leading industry events in your field. If you connect with the people who organize them, you can ask to be a part of these events. While you may not be a featured speaker, you may be able to serve on a panel. By associating yourself with this top industry event, you send the message that you, too, are an expert and a leader.

In closing...

One of my favorite quotes is from Oliver Wendall Holmes:

We all need an education in the obvious.

Is all of this Internet marketing stuff "obvious"? I suspect not! It is my hope that you will make Internet marketing a passionate study for you also. The Internet isn't about to go away anytime soon, and if you don't get a hold of it, you'll be left behind. I believe, though, that you are someone who is a "take charge" kind of person. Heck, you picked up this book, didn't you? Now, take the opportunity and implement these ideas. There are additional worksheets and resources available for you as well, in the back of this book. And, please, keep in touch with me. I love to hear and share Internet marketing success stories and it is my hope that one day I'll share your success with others. Thank you for allowing me the opportunity to serve you with the content of the pages of this book. May you be blessed with an abundance of success!

APPENDIX A:

WORKSHEETS

Product Launch Check-off Sheet

Final Check Off Sheet

To do an Internet marketing launch, you will have to keep track of many details. Before you set your product launch date, you should familiarize yourself with the entire strategy for your launch and be ready to get to work.

Assuming you've done that and are well into the process, the following is...

<u>Your final check-off sheet!</u>

Each item of this checklist is important and needs to be completed or at least considered if your launch is to be successful.

It is very important that you are on track and organized to be completely ready for your product launch. I suggest that approximately two weeks before you launch, you make a "Go" or "No Go" decision based on this assessment of your preparedness. You can always do the launch later when you are more prepared.

Listed below are the items you need to be able to answer YES to in order for you to be ready for a successful launch.

_____ Yes, I am familiar with the guidelines of the FTC and have abided by them to the letter, knowing that this launch is solely my responsibility. (See the Resources section for more information about FTC regulations.)

_____ Yes, I followed up **individually and personally** with everyone who is supporting me with my campaign as a partner and I have done so on a regular basis.

_____ Yes, I have received positive feedback (a phone call or a firm commitment in an e-mail) from all of my partners confirming their solo e-mail mailing(s) for my campaign.

_____ Yes, I've provided partners with plenty of notice for my campaign to give them time to schedule it into their agenda, and I have stayed in touch with them every week to be sure they haven't forgotten my chosen launch date and we are "good to go."

_____ Yes, I've asked every partner I've talked to if they know of anyone else who may be willing and/or able to help spread the word and become involved in my campaign.

_____ Yes, I plan to continue to look for partners right up to my campaign date and on the day of my campaign.

_____ Yes, I've identified my goals for my launch and I'm on track to meet them.

_____ Yes, the e-mail that my partners are sending on my behalf *and* my landing page copy/layout match all of the criteria needed for a compelling sales letter and everything looks great visually.

_____ Yes, I have additional support materials available and ready for my partners such as social media posts, long articles, and short excerpts that promote and shed light on the product/service I am launching.

_____ Yes, I've run my copy (e-mail, sales letter on the landing page, etc.) by others to check that it makes sense; it is clear and easy to understand and all the links are working.

_____ Yes, there are clear ordering instructions included in both my e-mail and landing page copy.

_____ Yes, all the links, forms to fill in, and auto-response e-mails that allow for the buyers to access the bonus gifts or free giveaways are working. (You can learn more about putting together bonus gift offerings in my book *Viral Explosions)*

_____ Yes, I have an announcement e-mail ready and have sent and received confirmation from my partners.

_____ Yes, I have short ads ready in the event I decide to use them.

_____ Yes, I've run my e-mail through known SPAM checkers to ensure it will not get caught in spam folders.

_____ Yes, I've checked that all links in the e-mails that will go out to my subscribers and to others' lists are working.

_____ Yes, I've provided my partners with the copy they need to send out for me on my campaign date and they have confirmed receipt.

_____ Yes, my product is ready and I have an ample supply.

_____ Yes, I have positive reviews and testimonials for my product and they are on my sales page.

_____ Yes, I have some bonuses that offer real value.

_____ Yes, my bonus gift bundle is unique and suited for my product. (Bundles are collections of bonus gifts offered by you and your partners. See _Viral Explosions_ for more details.)

_____ Yes, I have tested my download page where customers can retrieve their bonus gifts. All downloads and links work perfectly. (I have asked others to test it and all of the links are working properly for them too.)

_____ Yes, the instructions for accessing the bonuses are crystal clear.

_____ Yes, my campaign is for a limited time period to build a sense of urgency that gets people to buy now.

_____ Yes, I have blocked off the time in my agenda to respond to any e-mails as they come in.

_____ Yes, I've followed through on everything that needs to be done to make this a success.

Remember: If you are not ready to launch your campaign then by all means postpone it. Being organized is crucial for the success of any campaign. Cross your "T"s and dot your "I"s.

And always remember, your positive attitude is of utmost importance. Please make it your sincerest intention for your campaign to succeed. I encourage you to use effective online marketing tools and become intimate with the strategy.

Wishing you great success!

Peggy McColl

Internet Project Plan Checklist

Your Project Title:

_____

Launch Campaign

Objective: To create $x,xxx,xxx
in revenue from the sale of   Campaign Date:

_____   _____

Creator of Prod-   # of Partners
uct
                      _____   _____

Product Title   # of solo e-mails
                                              to go out
                      _____   _____

Buyers will go   # for additional
to##?#   reach##?##
                      _____   _____

Resources
(People, Tools,
Sites, etc.) ##?#   _____

Week #12	Your Name:	Overall Project On Track?
This week's objective:		
Action Items:		Completed √

Week #11	Your Name:		Overall Project On Track?

This week's objective:

Action Items:			Completed √

Week #10	Your Name:		Overall Project On Track?

This week's objective:

Action Items:			Completed √

Week #9	Your Name:	Overall Project On Track?
This week's objective:		
Action Items:		Completed √

Week #8	Your Name:	Overall Project On Track?
This week's objective:		
Action Items:		Completed √

Week #7	Your Name:	Overall Project On Track?
This week's objective:		
Action Items:		Completed √

Week #6	Your Name:	Overall Project On Track?
This week's objective:		
Action Items:		Completed √

Week #5	Your Name:	Overall Project On Track?
This week's objective:		
Action Items:		Completed √

Week #4	Your Name:	Overall Project On Track?
This week's objective:		
Action Items:		Completed √

Week #3	Your Name:	Overall Project On Track?
This week's objective:		
Action Items:		Completed √

Week #2	Your Name:	Overall Project On Track?
This week's objective:		
Action Items:		Completed √

Week #1	Your Name:	Overall Project On Track?
This week's objective:		
Action Items:		Completed √

Notes to Self:

Notes to Self:

Notes to Self:

APPENDIX B:

RESOURCES

In addition to checking out these resources, be sure to do web searches by keyword and ask people for referrals from professionals they use or sites they go to.

Peggy McColl's Web sites

http://destinies.com

http://viralexplosions.com

http://viralexplosions.com/blog

http://centerforviralmarketing.com

http://destinies.com/rich

http://twitter.com/peggymccoll

http://facebook.com/peggy.mccoll

Peggy's Facebook page:

http://www.facebook.com/peggymccollfans

Peggy's blog

http://viralexplosions.com/blog

Peggy's YouTube Channel

http://youtube.com/peggymccoll

Other books by Peggy McColl:

Recommended Social Media Sites

While there are many social media sites now, these four are the ones that I recommend to work with:

http://www.facebook.com

http://www.linkedin.com

http://www.twitter.com

http://www.youtube.com

FTC Guidelines

The Internet is connecting advertisers and marketers to customers from Boston to Bali with text, interactive graphics, video and audio. If you're thinking about advertising on the Internet, remember that many of the same rules that apply to other forms of advertising apply to electronic marketing. These rules and guidelines protect businesses and consumers—and help maintain the credibility of the Internet as an advertising medium. The Federal Trade Commission (FTC)

has prepared this guide to give you an overview of some of the laws it enforces.
http://business.ftc.gov/documents/bus28-advertising-and-marketing-Internet-rules-road

Hasmark Services

My sister, Judy O'Beirn's company; Hasmark Services expertise is providing effective, industry leading online marketing solutions for authors, publishers, professionals and experts who wish to create a prominent online presence to sell books, products and services.
http://hasmarkservices.com

Sites You'll Find Helpful When You're Developing Your Products

Audio and Video Products

http://mixiv.com/

Teleseminar Services

http://peggymccoll.audioacrobat.com

Webinar Services

http://maestroconference.com

http://www.maestromonth.com

http://www.gotomeeting.com

http://www.webex.com

http://www.thewebinarpros.com

Graphic Design
You can buy book jacket designs, Web site templates, and packaging designs at:
http://www.killercovers.com.

Audio and Video

You can download royalty-free video clips, animation, and photographs at these sites:

http://www.istockphoto.com

http://www.bigstockphoto.com

http://www.fotosearch.com

eBooks and Books

Several companies offer self-publishing and/or print-on-demand services and related services that can range from editing to e-mail and social media marketing campaigns:

http://www.xlibris.com

http://www.iuniverse.com

http://www.lulu.com

http://www.outskirtspress.com

http://www.createspace.com

eBook Listings Sites

You can upload your eBook to be accessed on the following sites.

http://www.amazon.com

http://www.bn.com

http://www.ebooks.com

http://www.free-ebooks.net

http://www.gutenberg.org

If you're unable to convert your Word document to a .pdf when you save the file for your eBook, you can use the application here:

Word to .pdf
http://www.doc2pdf.net/converter/

Cute Writer Download
http://www.softpedia.com/progDownload/Cute Writer-Download-12692.html

To register your book's copyright

U.S.:
http://www.copyright.gov

Canada:
http://www.cb-cda.gc.ca/info/registration-e.html

Australia:
http://www.copyright.org.au

UK:
http://www.copyrightservice.co.uk

Ghostwriters and Editors

You can find professional ghostwriters and editors at:

The American Society of Journalists and Authors http://www.asja.org

Nancy Peske

Nancy has ghostwritten some of my other books and she edited this one.
http://www.nancypeske.com

Christine Messier

Christine is a ghost blogger, but she also does editing and ghost writing.
http://yourvoiceinc.com

Professional Editors and Copyeditors

You can find other professional editors and copyeditors at:

http://www.the-efa.org

http://www.elance.com

Literary Agents

You can find lists of literary agents at:

http://www.agentquery.com

http://www.everyonewhosanyone.com

http://www.writers.net/agents.html

http://www.writers-free-reference.com/agents

Resources for Bloggers

Your Voice, Christine Messier
http://yourvoiceinc.com

Sites Helpful for Promotion and Publicity

Bradley Communications

Steve Harrison & Bill Harrison provide a variety of publications, services and training events for authors, experts, entrepreneurs, non-profit organizations, public relations professionals and others to help them build their business and secure media publicity. http://www.rtir.com

http://www.nationalpublicitysummit.com

http://www.reporterconnection.com

http://www.freepublicity.com

http://www.milliondollarauthorclub.com

More Helpful Marketing and Publishing Tips for Authors from Rick Frishman

Rick sends out tips for authors twice a week. You can sign up on his site.
http://www.rickfrishman.com/

Author 101 University
A 'live' event where you can learn from the experts in the field of book marketing and publishing. http://www.author101university.com/

Morgan James Publishing offers you the advantages of traditional publishing as well as the time-to-market benefits normally associated with self publishing.
http://publishing.morgan-james.com/

Services for Delivering Newsletters and eCourses

You'll need a list service to manage your e-mail list. Many of the shopping cart services include this feature but you can also use:

http://www.aweber.com

http://www.icontact.com

http://www.netatlantic.com

http://www.constantcontact.com

Shopping Cart Services

http://www.1shoppingcart.com

http://www.clickbank.com

Sites That Will Help You Identify Potential Affiliates

You can check the popularity of particular Web sites, which will help you identify potential affiliates, at:

http://alexa.com

http://compete.com

Sites That Will Help You with Web site Hosting and Design

The following are services that allow you to reserve a domain name and buy hosting services. Some offer you free Web site templates and design advice, too:

http://www.smallbusiness.yahoo.com

http://www.godaddy.com

http://www.networksolutions.com

http://www.intuit.com

http://godaddy.com

Web site Designer

Colin Miller

I recommend this Web site designer.
http://www.onegraphic.com

Free Web site Templates

This is a source for free Web site templates:
http://www.killersites.com

Author Instruction

These sites will help authors who want to get published.

Author U
http://authoru.org

The Book Shepherd for authors who want to create books that have no regrets.
http://thebookshepherd.com

Subscriber List Building

This site features a product that offers help in building a subscriber list.
http://www.trafficgeyser.com

Copywriters

Here are some copywriters you may want to study:

http://www.thegaryhalbertletter.com

http://www.tednicholas.com

http://www.dankennedy.com

http://www.davidgarfinkel.com

Article Submission Sites

The articles are made available to Web sites and e-mail newsletter owners looking for content. They usually have strict rules about how much promotional material can be included in the article but you can always insert a link to your Web site into your author biography if not the text of the article itself.

http://www.ezinearticles.com

http://www.articlesbase.com

http://www.Buzzle.com

http://www.GoArticles.com

http://www.ArticleAlley.com

http://www.ArticleDashboard.com

http://www.selfgrowth.com

http://www.articlemarketer.com

http://www.isnare.com

http://www.ideamarketers.com

http://www.articlecity.com

http://www.articlehub.com

http://www.articlesfactory.com

http://www.marketing-seek.com

http://www.goarticles.com

Press Releases Submission Sites

http://www.prweb.com

http://www.24-7pressrelease.com

http://www.prfree.com

http://www.prleap.com

http://www.przoom.com

http://www.pr.com

http://www.1888pressrelease.com

http://www.prlog.org

http://www.prnewswire.com

http://www.i-newswire.com

http://www.newswire.ca *(in Canada)*

Video Submission Sites

You can upload your video to these sites, where it can be accessed free of charge by anyone.

http://www.youtube.com

http://www.video.google.com

http://www.video.yahoo.com

http://www.atomfilms.com *(comedy only)*

http://www.twango.com

Media Opportunities Resources

You can learn about interview and media opportunities here:

Help a Reporter Out or HARO is a service that sends out requests for anecdotes, talk show guests, and experts that come in from journalists, freelance writers, bloggers, and television and radio producers. Subscribe to services like this one to scout for opportunities to promote your brand and product http://www.haro.com.

Their PR service will send out press releases as well as send you leads from reporters. http://www.prleads.com

GLOSSARY OF TERMS

Affiliate marketing. A marketing program or campaign that uses compensated partners to promote a product.

Affiliates. Partners in marketing who agree to promote a product, often, but not always, in return for a share of the revenue generated by sales of the product.

Blog piece. An essay or comment posted on a blog.

Blog. Short for web log, a blog is an online journal that allows the creator to post text, video, audio, and links, and invite comments from others. A blog can be self-standing or it can be connected to a Web site. "Blog" is also a verb: "I want to blog about that topic."

Co-writer. A co-writer shares the work of writing with another person. She receives public credit for her role (for example, if she co-writes a book, her name will appear on the cover).

Cookies. Also known as tracker cookies, these are bits of information stored on an Internet browser that allow a Web site to remember the settings it last used for the visitors. When you "clear cookies" on your browser, the information is erased. Cookies are used to record shopping cart contents, user IDs and passwords, and other information that the visitor might want to access upon his next visit.

Copyeditor. An editor whose duties include fact checking, correcting grammar and punctuation, and proofreading. A copyeditor does less rewriting and structuring than an editor typically does, so if both an editor and copyeditor are working on a book, the editor's work will be completed before the copyeditor begins his task.

Copywriter. A professional writer whose specialty is composing sales or advertising text, or copy.

e-mail subscriber list. A compilation of e-mail addresses and names of people who have contacted the e-mail list owner and agreed to be added to a list for receiving future e-mails. An e-mail subscriber list should not be confused with an e-mail list compiled by a third party, which generates *spam,* that is, e-mail communications that have not been requested by the recipient.

e-mail subscribers. People who have chosen to receive future e-mails from an e-mail list owner and provided their e-mail address and other information.

eBook. Short for *e*lectronic book, an eBook is a digital book. Although it may be in an Adobe .pdf format, for an eBook to be read on a computer, eReader, or smart phone, it must be formatted so that it can be read on that particular device.

eCourse. A series of e-mails sent to recipients to provide them with information in a sequential manner. An eCourse may also involve interaction with the students and homework, just as with an offline course.

Editor. An editor organizes, corrects, and condenses text. Editors who work at publishing houses (sometimes called *in-house editors*) or at periodicals will also have the duty of choosing material for publication and may or may not do the actual editing of the text.

eProduct. A digital, electronic product such as an audio, video, or electronic book.

eReader. A device for displaying eBooks so that they can be read, usually handheld. Kindle and Nook are popular eReaders. A smart phone can serve as an eReader as well.

Facebook. A popular social networking site, originally created for use by college students, where people can interact online and exchange information through various means including a personal "wall" where they and their Facebook friends can post short messages.

FTC. The Federal Trade Commission, a division of the U.S. government that regulates, oversees, and enforces rules regarding advertising and promotion in order to protect consumers.

Fulfillment house. A company that offers product storage, shipping, and related services to business owners.

Ghostwriter. A ghostwriter writes others' peoples books, articles, and reports for them and does not receive public credit for her work. The term "ghost" refers to the fact that her role in the writing is invisible to the public.

Hosting service. A company that provides the bandwidth for maintaining a site on the world wide web. Most hosting services have their own servers and offer extra services such as Web site templates and the ability to secure domain names.

Information-based product. A product, or package of services, where the value lies in the information, guidance, and advice provided. A book is an information-based product. An eBook is an information-based eProduct.

Landing page or sales page. A page on the Internet that is freestanding with its own web address or that is attached to a Web site or blog, a landing page contains sales copy and links.

LinkedIn. A social networking site, originally designed for professionals seeking to interact with other professionals.

Internet server. Hardware and software combined that provides users with the ability to host Web sites in virtual reality. A server may be used by more than one host.

Spam. E-mail or other electronic communication that has not been requested or solicited by the receiver. Spam e-mail is sometimes called "junk e-mail."

Streaming. Data transfer that sends digital information in a steady "stream." Audio or video files that play using streaming software do not download to your computer when they play.

Teleseminar. Short for a **tele**phone **seminar.** The presenter secures a teleconference line through a service and has attendees dial in at a predetermined time to participate in this live event.

Twitter. A social networking site where users can post very short messages called "Tweets.

Viral explosion. An extremely rapid spread of information via the Internet that yields extraordinary results

Voiceover Internet protocol. A service that allows people to utilize Internet connections to communicate in real time via audio and video. Skype is the most well-known voiceover Internet protocol.

Wall. Some social media sites feature a web page that is controlled by you, often called a "wall." Anyone who is who is part of your network can post on your wall and read the posts. You have the ability to delete posts, respond to them, or begin a dialogue and invite others to respond by posting on your "wall."

Webinar. Short for **Web**-based sem**inar.** A presentation, lecture, or workshop that's transmitted over the Internet and which allows the attendee to see the presenter, and any of her presentation materials, in real time.

YouTube. A video sharing site on the Internet.

ABOUT

THE

AUTHOR

PEGGY MCCOLL

Peggy McColl is a *New York Times* best-selling author. She has authored seven books which, between them, have been translated into more than 30 languages and are sold in over 80 countries in the world. Peggy is also an internationally recognized expert in the field of personal and professional development and Internet marketing.

As an entrepreneur, business owner, mentor, and professional speaker Peggy has been inspiring individuals to pursue their personal and business objectives and achieve ultimate success.

She provides effective Internet marketing solutions for entrepreneurs, authors, publishers, professionals, and business owners who want to establish an online presence, achieve best-seller status, build their brand, and grow or expand their business online. You can find out more about Peggy through her main Web site http://destinies.com. She lives in Ottawa, Ontario, Canada with her husband Denis and her son Michel (and her two adorable doggies Pablo and Noelle).

Additional Titles in The 99 Series®

99 Things You Wish You Knew Before...
Facing Life's Challenges
Filling Out Your Hoops Bracket
Going Into Debt
Going Into Sales
Ignoring the Green Revolution
Landing Your Dream Job
Losing Fat 4 Life
Making It BIG In Media
Marketing On the Internet
Taking Center Stage

99 Things Women Wish They Knew Before...
Dating After 40, 50, and YES, 60!
Getting Behind the Wheel of Their Dream Job
Getting Fit Without Hitting the Gym
Entering the World of Internet Dating
Falling In Love
Hitting Retirement
Starting Their Own Business

99 Things Parents Wish They Knew Before...
Cyberstalking Victimized Their Children
Having "THE" Talk

99 Things Brides Wish They Knew Before Planning Their Wedding

www.99-Series.com

9 780986 692390